Cultural Mediation for Museums

This book presents an innovative application of strategic and experiential marketing in the museum sector, which uses a new cultural mediation model to enrich the visitor experience via increased audience engagement.

Leveraging a case study of the National Gallery of Modern and Contemporary Arts in Rome, the book helps readers understand how to apply marketing management to cultural mediation, enabling museums to segment the visitors' market to drive improvements to arts accessibility and engagement. By running a comprehensive and multi-method research project, the authors propose a customized cultural mediation model to support museums in facing the current challenges and build their future. Our model supports museums in segmenting the visitors' market and designing cultural mediation for enriched visitor experiences; readers will also learn how to invest, manage, hire, and train staff members devoted to this service, resulting in more engaging and successful experiences.

This book will be a valuable resource for educational services offices at museums worldwide. This book will also be of interest to researchers, academics, and scholars carrying out research in the fields of museum management, cultural mediation and communication, and marketing.

Michela Addis is Full Professor in Business Administration and Management at Università di Roma Tre, Italy.

Isabella de Stefano is an Art Historian and Head of Communication and Education at the National Gallery of Modern and Contemporary Art in Rome.

Valeria Guerrisi is an Architect and Research Fellow at the Center of Excellence – Cultural Technological District of Lazio Region, Italy.

Routledge Focus on the Global Creative Economy
Series Editor: Aleksandar Brkić, Goldsmiths, University of London, UK

This innovative Shortform book series aims to provoke and inspire new ways of thinking, new interpretations, emerging research, and insights from different fields. In rethinking the relationship of creative economies and societies beyond the traditional frameworks, the series is intentionally inclusive. Featuring diverse voices from around the world, books in the series bridge scholarship and practice across arts and cultural management, the creative industries and the global creative economy.

Innovation in the Arts
Concepts, Theories, and Practices
Jason C. White

Creative Women in Ireland
Not Your Muse
Aileen O'Driscoll

Cultural Mediation for Museums
Driving Audience Engagement
Edited by Michela Addis, Isabella de Stefano, and Valeria Guerrisi

For more information about this series, please visit: www.routledge.com/Routledge-Focus-on-the-Global-Creative-Economy/book-series/RFGCE

Cultural Mediation for Museums

Driving Audience Engagement

Edited by
Michela Addis, Isabella de Stefano,
and Valeria Guerrisi

Routledge
Taylor & Francis Group

LONDON AND NEW YORK

First published 2023
by Routledge
4 Park Square, Milton Park, Abingdon, Oxon OX14 4RN

and by Routledge
605 Third Avenue, New York, NY 10158

Routledge is an imprint of the Taylor & Francis Group, an informa business

British Library Cataloguing-in-Publication Data
A catalogue record for this book is available from the British Library

Library of Congress Cataloging-in-Publication Data
Names: Addis, Michela, editor. | De Stefano, Isabella, editor. | Guerrisi, Valeria, editor. (To be estab)
Title: Cultural mediation for museums : driving audience engagement / edited by Michela Addis, Isabella de Stefano, and Valeria Guerrisi.
Description: Abingdon, Oxon; New York, NY : Routledge, 2023. | Series: Routledge focus on the global creative economy | Includes bibliographical references and index.
Identifiers: LCCN 2022048569 (print) | LCCN 2022048570 (ebook) | ISBN 9781032403694 (hbk) | ISBN 9781032403700 (pbk) | ISBN 9781003352754 (ebk)
Subjects: LCSH: Museum visitors—Case studies. | Cultural competence—Case studies. | Communication in museums—Case studies. | Museums—Management—Case studies. | Galleria nazionale d'arte moderna (Italy)—Case studies.
Classification: LCC AM7.C855 2023 (print) | LCC AM7 (ebook) | DDC 069/.1—dc23/eng/20221021
LC record available at https://lccn.loc.gov/2022048569
LC ebook record available at https://lccn.loc.gov/2022048570

ISBN: 978-1-032-40369-4 (hbk)
ISBN: 978-1-032-40370-0 (pbk)
ISBN: 978-1-003-35275-4 (ebk)

DOI: 10.4324/9781003352754

Typeset in Times New Roman
by codeMantra

Contents

Figures

Tables

Contributors

Michela Addis is a Full Professor in Business Administration and Management at Università di Roma Tre, Italy. She holds a PhD in "Business Economics & Management" from Bocconi University – Milan (2001). She currently coordinates the research infrastructure of the Center of Excellence – Cultural Technological District of Lazio Region, Italy. Her research interests include experiential marketing, hedonic consumption, branding, arts, and cultural marketing. Some of her publications appeared in the *Journal of Consumer Research, Journal of Service Research, Journal of Cultural Economics, Psychology & Marketing,* and *European Journal of Marketing.* For Taylor and Francis – Routledge, she recently published *Engaging Brands* (2020) and coedited *Managing the Cultural Businesses: Avoiding Mistakes, Finding Success* (2021). She currently serves as Associate Editor in Strategic Marketing and Consumer Behavior in the Arts for the *International Journal of Arts Management.*

Walter Altamirano Aguilar is a student in Economics of Cultural and Creative Industries at the University of Roma Tre. In 2019, he participated in the Lazio Region's scholarship program, Torno Subito. In 2020, he participated in Dock3 Lab, a startup incubator at Roma Tre, by running a startup project dedicated to roman artistic craftsmanship: "Artem". In 2021, he got a university internship at the National Gallery of Modern Art in Rome conducting market research and analysis on the figure of cultural mediation.

Rosina Baldo has a degree in Economics of Cultural and Creative Industries from the University of Roma Tre. In 2021, she got a university internship at the National Gallery of Modern Art in Rome conducting market research and analysis on the figure of cultural mediation. She is now working as a community manager in a former startup, which is a company in the insurance industry that collaborates with insurance companies in claims management.

Valeria Bellusci is a student in Economics of Cultural and Creative Industries at the University of Roma Tre. In 2020, she co-authored the paper *Social Inequality and Gender Discrimination: An Investigation in the Territory of Rome* (MappaRoma publishing). In 2021, she got a university internship at the National Gallery of Modern Art in Rome conducting market research and analysis on the figure of cultural mediation.

Isabella de Stefano is an art historian. She has a degree in Art History, a postgraduate specialization in modern and contemporary art, and a master's degree in communication and management in public administration. Her research interest and publications include communication, cultural mediation, and inclusive projects of art education. She has been working for the Italian Ministry of Culture since 2000, previously in communication and public relations, from 2018 she is Head of Communication and Education at the National Gallery of Modern and Contemporary Art in Rome.

Zoe Giannotti is a student in Political Economy at the University of Roma Tre. Since 2019, she has been one of the founding partners of Pop-Olio, a social promotion association that operates on a national basis to increase and enhance olive oil production awareness. Since 2020, she has been the social media manager of Tedaldi, an Italian company that promotes sustainable production. In 2021, she got a university internship at the National Gallery of Modern Art in Rome conducting market research and analysis on the figure of cultural mediation. She is currently working as a strategy manager in Mirage Studio Design.

Valeria Guerrisi is an architect. She is currently a research fellow at the Center of Excellence – Cultural Technological District of Lazio Region, Italy. In 2020, she accomplished a biennial master's degree in "Heritage: knowledge, preservation, valorization, management" at the University of Roma Tre. She was a research assistant in the Laboratory of Cultural Marketing at the University of Roma Tre (2019–2021). She is a partner of the Warehouse of Architecture and Research, with extended experience in the field of cultural heritage and cultural events. Since 2019, she has been the editorial coordinator of the architectural magazine Panteon.

Anna Minici has a Bachelor's degree in Economics and Business Management from the University of Roma Tre. Currently she is a master's student in Economics and Management with a specialization in marketing at the University of Roma Tre. In 2021, she got a university internship at the National Gallery of Modern Art in Rome conducting market research and analysis on the figure of cultural mediation.

Preface

The most relevant resource for museums is their audience. The new definition of museums released in August 2022 by ICOM, the International Council of Museums, puts at the core their activities "in the service of society" through the offering of "varied experiences for education, enjoyment, reflection and knowledge sharing". The audience actively contributes to creating experiences, but their engagement remains a difficult challenge for museums.

Especially the recent pandemic has shown that museums face multiple difficulties in reaching and engaging their visitors, making their engagement a top priority. To that end, cultural mediation is a key driver to make arts accessible even to the most distant visitors. Thus, cultural mediation has raised the interest of many museums. Traditionally cultural organizations design mediation in accord with "the one-best solution" principle, providing one single concept of cultural mediation to the entire audience. However, this model does not work out, and better cultural mediation services can be designed to increase audience engagement. But how? To solve this issue, as marketing management teaches, museums should segment their visitors' market, and design accordingly cultural mediation.

This book explains how to adopt this customizing strategy. Based on a multi-method research project run in 2021 by the University of Roma Tre for (and in collaboration with) the National Gallery of Modern and Contemporary Arts in Rome, this book presents a marketing management model to tailor cultural mediation according to visitors' profiles for the benefits of museums' educational services offices.

Chapter 1 focuses on the processes of cultural mediation adopted at the National Gallery of Modern and Contemporary Art in Rome. Isabella de Stefano, Head of Communication and Education at the National Gallery of Modern and Contemporary Art, presents the challenges that the Gallery has to deal with and how cultural mediation helps the museum in engaging visitors.

Chapter 2 presents the state of the art of studies related to audience engagement in the arts. After providing the definition, Michela Addis identifies the drivers of audience engagement. Among them, the visitor's ability to fully immerse in the experience is a key driver that cultural organizations must leverage. By providing visitors with useful, enriched, and customized information, museums design labels, apps, and cultural mediation to engage them. Thus, audience engagement emerges as the ultimate goal of museum cultural mediation.

After the setting of the goal of museum cultural mediation, Chapter 3 presents the state of the art of this service for the benefit of visitors. Starting with the results of a multidisciplinary literature review about museum cultural mediation, Zoe Giannotti focuses on managerial practices. By discussing the findings of two benchmarking analyses run on 33 educational programs worldwide and 68 worldwide examples of museum cultural mediation, a list of the competencies and skills needed for cultural mediation emerges.

Although knowing the state of the art about museum cultural mediation is important, certainly it is not enough to design more engaging experiences. Toward that goal, a comprehensive understanding of the visitors' point of view is needed. Chapter 4 addresses this topic. By leveraging in-depth interviews with visitors who experience museum cultural mediation for the first time, Rosina Baldo and Anna Minici identify the visitors' value chains regarding the museum cultural mediation, depicting four different visitor profiles.

The following Chapter 5 builds on the full set of findings presented and proposes an innovative model. Different cultural mediators target different visitors' profiles. Walter Altamirano Aguilar and Valeria Bellusci suggest a customized model of museum cultural mediation able to satisfy both the needs of the museum and visitors and achieve audience engagement. Four kinds of cultural mediators – namely, the Guide, the Educator, the Designer, and the Manager Mediators – differ regarding their education, key skills, communication abilities, and target audience; each of them satisfies the need of a specific target profile.

Finally, Chapter 6 focuses on the organizational structures that sustain cultural mediation. As Valeria Guerrisi explains, this educational service can be fully explored only if the museums (1) set up a clear audience development strategy; (2) design a proper organizational structure; (3) know their visitors; and (4) customize their cultural mediation offerings.

Together, the six chapters contribute to better designing museum cultural mediation. However, each of them is self-standing, addressing a specific step of this strategy making cultural mediation easier and more effective from the managerial, organizational, and operational points of view.

Acknowledgments

Although the ideas presented in this book are to be attributed to the authors of the individual chapters, they frequently originate in the many debates we have had with our students, managers, and members of the educational staff who daily contribute to generating value in these areas. It is therefore to them that our first big thank you goes. Our gratitude first goes to Cristiana Collu, director of the National Gallery of Modern and Contemporary Art, for her competence, effort, and extraordinary passion that puts into her work. For the same reason, we would like to mention Cecilia Casorati, director of Accademia di Belle Arti in Rome, who constantly receives and accepts the invitation to collaborate with the National Gallery of Modern and Contemporary Art for the success of the mediation service, by training and stipulating internship programs. Last but not least, our special thanks go to the mediators of the National Gallery, whose experience has provided much food for thought, and to the visitors who actively participated in the research project presented in this book.

1 Introduction

Isabella de Stefano

Rome's National Gallery of Modern and Contemporary Art hosts 20,000 works including paintings, drawings, sculptures, and installations and offers a great panorama on art starting from the nineteenth century. It is a museum of research and experimentation where anybody and everybody can reflect on language, exhibition experiences, and the role of contemporary museums.

Every year the museum organizes many international and important exhibitions. The concept of cultural mediation took off at the National Gallery in 2018, in the exhibition *BRIC-à- brac – The Jumble of Growth* 另一种选择.

In this exhibition, curated by Huang Du and Gerardo Mosquera (July 17–October 14, 2018), about 40 works by 26 international artists were shown.

The presence of many works created by Chinese artists provided the National Gallery with the opportunity to propose not only cultural but also linguistic mediation to the public. The exhibition would also attract Chinese tourists, with the possibility of offering tours in Chinese appealing not only to them but also to Chinese communities living in Rome and in Italy.

The problem, however, was where and how to find cultural mediators who spoke Chinese.

The National Gallery launched a quick survey to find Chinese cultural mediators and, in order to strengthen its relationships within the territory, directed its attention to the closest universities and cultural institutes to the museum. From an analysis of the territorial context, it emerged that the Academy of Fine Arts of Rome, located nearby in the centre in via di Ripetta, had many male and female Chinese students among its student body. In addition, the Academy of Fine Arts also included training internships to be carried out in museums as part of the curriculum for enrolled students.

DOI: 10.4324/9781003352754-1

In agreement with the director of the National Gallery, Cristiana Collu, the museum began a collaboration with the Academy of Fine Arts and entered into an agreement with the Academy for male and female students to carry out training internships, aimed at conducting cultural mediation visits in the museum's exhibition spaces. In this way, the Academy's students would continue their educational experience at the museum and, at the same time, offer cultural mediation visits to the public. Their proximity turned out to be very useful, because the students were able to easily walk to the museum after finishing their classes at the Academy.

The Academy, at the request of the National Gallery, publishes an annual call for applications, from October to November. Since 2018, more than 150 students have taken part in the cultural mediation initiative and responded to the call for applications. The National Gallery, in agreement with the Academy of Fine Arts, has selected 50 students every year, who expressed a desire to carry out cultural mediation internships from January to December.

Some students were so enthusiastic that they have taken part in the cultural mediation initiative at the National Gallery twice during their training at the Academy.

Among the requirements of the call for applications are knowledge of foreign languages, especially English, a good record regarding exams, up-to-date payment of university fees, and successfully passing the Contemporary Art exam.

Cultural mediation training takes place both in the classroom, led by teachers from the Academy, and directly in the field, at the National Gallery, in collaboration with the head of the Education Department of the National Gallery. Training is also managed by mediators who have participated in mediation in previous years and represent an important channel to learn about the museum, its spaces, and its people.

Mediators are on site at the Gallery during every day the museum is open, from Tuesday to Sunday, throughout the year. They conduct tours with all types of audience, including children, families, teenagers, the elderly, and audiences with disabilities.

They are recognizable because they wear a white t-shirt, with a blue "Ask a Mediator" logo. They wait for visitors at the entrance, near the ticket office.

Mediators are not tour guides and differ from them because they conduct a visit that is not limited only to the knowledge of the artwork and its creator. The goal of mediation is to interact and enter into a dialogue with the visiting public in front of the works of art, to arouse the visitor's curiosity, to prompt questions, and to invite them to interpret the work of art according to their point of view, with the support of the tools offered through mediation.

The meaning of the word cultural mediation can be encapsulated in a few actions: walk, converse, know, observe, and include.

These actions describe a dynamic, active (i.e. non-passive) attitude that characterizes cultural mediation visits, where integration and especially the relationship between the one who speaks and the one who listens takes on a fundamental importance. Mediation is a mutual exchange, which goes beyond the model of vertical communication where the expert speaks, and the visitor silently listens.

Mediation is dialogue and listening at the same time: the mediator speaks, the audience listens, but also the visitor speaks and the mediator listens. The mediator's listening to the audience is active listening without judgment. Mediators report that they have also learned about the National Gallery and its works through the questions and reflections shared with the audience.

The verb "walk" also contributes to a better understanding of cultural mediation.

In fact, the mediator is never stationary, but their dynamic attitude is reflected in an interaction not only with the visitor but also with the works and the space. The mediator does not describe the works in a frontal position but must be able to speak by moving around the work, shifting the observer's point of view and perception, and inviting them to look at the work from different perspectives.

Mediation is also an invitation to observe. The mediator pushes the visitor towards "slow looking," so that the visitor can intensely observe the work, in an attempt to interpret and get to know it not only from their point of view, but also through the other person's point of view and knowledge.

Mediation also means inclusion, because a mediation visit presupposes not only the mediator's narrative and perception but also that of the visitor who talks and converses, providing and sharing with the mediator their perceptions before the artwork.

Mediation visits are aimed at all the audiences that visit the museum and do not require reservations. In fact, they are free of charge and in high demand because contemporary art is very often not easily understandable or accessible to everyone.

In addition, the National Gallery's new exhibition design, *Time is Out Of Joint,* for the first time presents the permanent collection as an exhibition about time and introduces visitors to a free tour itinerary, unshackled from spatial and temporal limitations. With this new and original arrangement, starting from 2016 to today, the general public has been able to choose its own personal visiting itinerary and, now free to walk through the spaces without being constrained to a pre-defined route, appreciates and requests mediation to delve into the details of a work or to enquire about the concept behind this important and significant curatorial choice. With *Time is Out of Joint,* mediation is crucial because in this free itinerary the visitor can become disoriented and in need of information about the artworks, the artists and the concept behind the museum's new exhibition design.

Unlike traditional guided tours, which have pre-defined time frames, a mediation visit is tailored to the visitor's needs, so every time is different from the last. It can last from five minutes to two hours. It is the audience that decides, based on their time availability and preferences, what to see and for how long.

There is no defined itinerary in the mediation, but from time to time the route changes according to the demands and preferences of the audience. Some may prefer figurative works, while others opt for abstract works. In mediation, the visit is free not only in time but also in space.

Mediation presupposes horizontal communication that is based on a peer-to-peer dialogue between the mediator and the visitor. Peer-to-peer dialogue works very well with teens and young audiences who tend to prefer horizontal, interactive communication. High school work placement projects, in which high school students work alongside mediators in the field and learn the communication techniques behind cultural mediation, demonstrate the effectiveness of horizontal communication with this age group, in particular. According to internal data of the National Gallery, teens often prefer to listen to and learn information from their peers, whom they trust and whose authority they recognize.

Through the mediators, the National Gallery has also designed "site-specific" projects aimed at specific targets.

My masterpiece includes cultural mediation visits to primary and secondary schools. At the end of the visit, mediators ask the children to do a drawing of the artwork that impressed them the most during their visit to the Gallery.

Community is aimed at foreign communities living in Italy and consists of a series of cultural mediation visits in various languages, including English, French, German, Chinese, and Russian. The students from the British School at Rome, at the end of their visit to the National Gallery, told us *"the museum is committed to engaging the public and you choose great mediators to achieve this"* (internal data).

The Artist is Me is aimed at adolescents with psychiatric and behavioural disorders while *I Feed on Art* is aimed mainly at girls with eating disorders. Both projects consist of visits and creative workshops in front of works of art, with the aim of making museum activities also part of the mental and physical rehabilitation pathways provided in adolescents' recovery.

Metamorphosis is a project of visits and cultural mediation meetings aimed at the boys and girls in the Casal del Marmo juvenile prison in Rome.

Since mediators are in close contact with the public and their presence is one of the distinguishing features of the National Gallery, for the Education Department of the National Gallery the need to monitor the quality of visits conducted by cultural mediators is crucial. That is the only way to analyse the strengths and weaknesses of cultural mediation.

To that end, a comprehensive research project has been designed at the National Gallery that began in 2019. It aims not only to identify the profile of the mediator that most closely matches the needs of the National Gallery but also to outline the optimal model of cultural mediation.

I am particularly happy that the National Gallery has been chosen as a reference for the investigation and study of the model of cultural mediation.

Much progress has been made at the National Gallery since 2018 but there is still much to do, and undoubtedly this volume will provide invaluable support in overcoming any critical issues that the surveys may highlight.

In fact, this volume will be very useful to all those who will decide to pursue a career in cultural mediation, not only at the National Gallery but at all museums and galleries around the world. It will also provide an effective study tool for students and all those in the field who wish to deepen their knowledge and understanding of cultural mediation, perhaps experiencing it for the first time at the museums where they work.

This is my wish and my conviction.

2 Audience Engagement, Its Drivers, and Its Implications for Museum Cultural Mediation

Michela Addis

2.1 Audience Engagement: The Ultimate Goal of Museums

The recent Covid-19 pandemic has highlighted several important vulnerabilities in museums' value creation and value delivery processes (UNESCO 2020). Museums are subject to unprecedented pressure because they must quickly learn how to approach the public in completely new ways. Regardless of country, governance, size, collection, or any other differing detail, almost all museums have been severely affected by closures and restrictions. The vast majority of museums (estimated at approximately 75%) have registered a loss in revenue from €1,000 up to €30,000 per week but for larger European museums, the figure can reach between €100,000 and €600,000 per week of closure (NEMO 2020, 2021). In the US, the situation is similar with museums collectively losing a minimum of $33 million every day they were closed (American Alliance of Museums 2020).

Reopening, however, is not the ultimate cure. To recover from the pandemic and to address again their highly dynamic environment, museums have to reinvent their business models, as both ICOM (2020) and UNESCO (2020) have promptly suggested. In order to reach this goal, a market-oriented approach is essential in these challenging environments (Falk and Dierking 2016). The role of arts organizations is shifting from the perspective of mastery to one of service (Weil 1997). Arts organizations are increasingly becoming experience-centred institutions based on audience, individual needs, and personal significance (Weil 1997). Museums have progressively changed their role, distancing themselves from their role as 'guardians of high-brow culture' and shifting instead towards a more commercial position in the leisure market. Museums urgently need a fresh strategy to increase their appeal and create superior service delivery, but they are typically

DOI: 10.4324/9781003352754-2

unfamiliar with its design (Carù and Cuadrado 2020). When this is the case, a stronger focus on the ultimate goal of every museum – namely, audience engagement – might provide the answer to such a difficult question both for museums (Venkatesh and Meamber 2006; Kemp 2015) and policymakers.

A deeper understanding of audience engagement and its drivers is the starting point of any strategy for establishing, maintaining, and developing visitor relationships. Nowadays, this is especially important because digital and other emerging technologies offer a broad range of solutions to enrich artistic experiences, with many different examples worldwide that need a more comprehensive analysis in order to fulfil their promise. Invariably, only truly engaged customers are willing to share their knowledge and participate in activities and new experiences. Indeed, customers are clearly key strategic sources of knowledge for anyone interested in developing and reinforcing their competitive advantage (Addis and Holbrook 2001; Shaw and Williams 2009; Sørensen and Jensen 2015). Therefore, a comprehensive understanding of audience engagement and its drivers is especially critical for museum educators (Wood and Wolf 2008) who have to understand that, to increase audience engagement, museums need to design experiences that unite education, entertainment, and commitment (Barab 2006), by focusing on the visitors, the learning environment, and the conceptual understanding that they want to convey (Wood and Wolf 2008).

2.2 Defining Audience Engagement and Its Drivers

Over time, scholars from many fields have investigated and explored audience engagement, contributing to defining it as the key driver of cultural organizations' success (Wood and Wolf 2008). Every cultural organization today aims to reach larger and more diversified audiences. However, despite its key relevance and its widespread popularity, its conceptualization still requires attention (Carnwath and Brown 2014). Specifically, although everyone mostly agrees on the benefits of audience engagement for arts and cultural organizations (Kemp 2015), its drivers remain somewhat elusive. What is clear is that engagement is based on compelling, customized, and open-ended experiences, as in any other industry (Black 2005; Addis 2020). According to marketing studies, engagement is a "psychological state" (Brodie et al. 2011), which results from highly interactive, dynamic, co-creative, and relational customer experiences. Since the interactions between a customer (i.e. a visitor in the arts and cultural industry) and a brand are both direct and indirect, they are innumerable throughout the relationship span. Consequently, the features of these interactions are crucial in driving audience engagement (Mujtaba et al. 2018).

Indeed, leveraging the four kinds of interactive touchpoints that start customer experiences but differ in terms of control (Lemon and Verhoef 2016), museum audience engagement results from an interactive process depending on:

- **Museum-owned touchpoints**. Museums typically design specific touchpoints that are under their full control. For instance, exhibition centres define the labels for their pieces of art, the physical entrance doors, the lighting system, and so forth. They are all influenced by their strategic goals.
- **Partner-owned touchpoints**. This category is less controllable by the museums since they depend on their partners. Common examples include partnering influencers in the digital environment, not owned points of sale, posts by communications agencies, and interactions with the partner's staff.
- **Visitor-owned touchpoints**. Touchpoints in this category are owned directly by the visitors and are under their own responsibility. Physical or digital word of mouth, user-generated content, and so on are typical examples in this category.
- **Other-owned touchpoints**. Finally, touchpoints that are under the control of others belong to this category (others can be, for instance, experts, critics, journalists, other museums, etc.).

Regardless of their category, touchpoints are the interactive platform for the visitor experiences. Thus, engagement is the layered result of the visitor experience over time, in a never-ending progression; it is therefore highly dynamic, adjusting easily and quickly. When these experiences are designed coherently and consistently over time, engagement increases, and likewise, its multiple benefits. Understanding its drivers is a relevant topic because they represent the managerial tools to leverage in order to reach higher levels of success (Brodie et al. 2011; Addis 2020). To identify the antecedents of audience engagement, marketing studies provide a useful perspective: audience engagement relates to the market approach. Arts marketing academics started to explore cultural consumption experiences in the 1980s (Colbert and St. James 2014), defining engagement in the arts as the emotive, cognitive, and relational responses evoked by aesthetic experiences (Kemp 2015). However, arts institutions still today do not possess adequate tools or information to define the appropriate strategies to promote the participation of their targets (Addis and Rurale 2020). By leveraging the marketing literature (Hollebeek 2011; Addis 2020), there are three categories of drivers of audience engagement:

1 Museum-based drivers
2 Visitor-based drivers
3 Context-based drivers

2.2.1 Museum-Based Drivers

Museums play a key role in designing cultural experiences to raise audience engagement. Indeed, they focus on several key variables.

- **Offerings.** First, their offerings are a key variable to design. Museums provide their visitors with tangible goods, intangible services, and, more generally, cultural experiences. In any case, museums, along with other cultural organizations, play with important emotional contents, featuring hedonic consumption.
- **Entertainment.** One of the most common variables to drive audience engagement is entertainment, which greatly affects experiences in many industries. Indeed, entertainment is not only a specific industry (Hennig-Thurau and Houston 2019) but its contents enrich engaging relationships with customers across industries. Museums are especially involved in this widespread entertainment content which has given rise to the concept of edutainment, i.e. the convergence of education and entertainment (Addis 2005).
- **Communication.** Communication has always been a key variable for museums to the extent that it usually represents the bulk of their marketing investment. Communication is quite powerful in creating engaging experiences that can even begin before a visit to a museum. Emotional messages greatly contribute to creating engaging experiences, with a relevant impact on individual attitudes and preferences. Specifically, images and videos can make messages go viral, and museums can actively benefit from privileged scenarios made up of inspirational images and content. Furthermore, marketing and communication managers know that the entire below-the-line area (such as events, sponsorships, social media, and guerrilla marketing) represents a powerful collection of tools to engage visitors.
- **Distance.** Museums propose offerings that differ in terms of individual perceived distance. Every individual shows a different level of cultural capital, resulting from the accumulation of experiences that have been stratified over time. Clearly, cultural capital exerts

a strong influence on individual attitudes and preferences towards arts and when museums do not leverage this cultural capital, or when individuals show limited cultural capital, the museum is often perceived as distant, detached from individual well-being. This perceived distance might intimidate visitors, and this is what typically happens in science and contemporary arts, where the level of difficulty of the cultural experience is perceived as high with people often imagining they will have trouble understanding and comprehending it (Doyle 2013). In these cases, a "comprehensive arts education" is needed to understand works of art, thus driving audience engagement.

- **Co-creation.** Highly interactive cultural experiences increase audience engagement, and research suggests that consumer attitudes, tastes, and preferences towards the art market are changing. Customers prefer cultural offerings that include active participation, interaction, and, if possible, co-creation (Styvén 2010). Co-creation can thus become a key driver of audience engagement, both in the value creation and value delivery processes (Addis 2020). Indeed, a deeper understanding of consumer interactions and relationships with artworks is essential to developing an immersive and transformative discourse (Goulding 2000) where repeated visitor experiences can shape relationships in the long term. At the same time, every participant contributes actively and individually to co-creative value processes: an individual who does not act as a "prosumer" cannot be engaged. To achieve that goal, flexible processes must be designed to face and manage uncertainty. The relevance of active participation has recently increased due to the Covid pandemic, for two key reasons. The first refers to the fact that individuals are eager to satisfy their social needs and a sense of unity. The isolation created by lockdowns and more generally by policies designed to limit the spread of Covid has increased the need for reducing social distance. The second refers to the large investment made in technological solutions in the arts and cultural industries worldwide, facilitating a participatory market approach.

2.2.2 Visitor-Based Drivers

A second key category of drivers of audience engagement relates to visitors that are the key characters in highly subjective experiences. As reality is necessarily subjective, dynamic, and personal, every individual has different experiences. Hundreds of individual variables have been studied and embedded in our personal history and lives.

- **Goals.** For individuals, consumption is a means to reaching their goals. This is the final motivation, and these goals differ greatly in terms of intensity, awareness, nature, probability of achievement, temporal perspective, and individuality. Due to this broad range of goals, a multiplicity of concepts exists, e.g. reasons, needs, desires, goals, and wishes. They cover the cognitive, affective, reflective, and recreational dimensions. Museums should also keep the heterogeneous motivations of consumers and their evolution under control. Cultural experiences are typically hedonic consumptions, which are an end in themselves.
- **Personality features.** The five-factor model of personality – widely known as the "big five" – is a multifactorial concept that describes key personality traits. These features are openness to experience, conscientiousness, extraversion, agreeableness, and neuroticism. They empirically drive individual attitudes and preferences: for instance, being open to experience captures originality, imaginative capacity, breadth of interests, and the courage of individuals, and they are all drivers of audience engagement.
- **Nostalgia proneness.** Whenever cultural experience is grounded in the past, both historical and personal (Stern 1992), nostalgia proneness emerges as a key driver of audience engagement. Indeed, everyone has a greater or lesser propensity to indulge in nostalgic attitudes, which results in differing interpretations of the arts. The past offers huge opportunities to leverage the fascination of memory but to reach this goal the level of nostalgia proneness of potential and actual visitors must be ascertained.
- **Involvement.** Involvement is an internal state of arousal, which expresses the importance that an object/experience has for the individual (Zaichkowsky 1994). It is a dynamic concept that strongly influences individual choices.
- **Emotions and mood.** Almost 40 years ago, marketing scholars highlighted the essential role of the emotional sphere in aesthetic experiences, generating innate enjoyment and pleasure (Holbrook and Hirschman 1982). Indeed, hedonic consumption greatly differs from utilitarian consumption, which is a means to an end. Nowadays, after an impressive number of studies, emotional value is still regarded as a key dimension driving cultural consumption and audience engagement (Venkatesh and Meamber 2006; Colbert and St-James 2014).

- **Prior knowledge.** By prior knowledge, we mean an aggregated system of previous knowledge that any individual might have regarding specific cultural experiences. These typically leverage prior knowledge when interacting with the market. Prior knowledge includes familiarity and expertise, which can be acquired by direct or indirect, previous experiences.

2.2.3 Context-Based Drivers

The last driver category groups together any element related to physical, digital, and social environments where the individual-brand interaction takes place. Thus, by "context" we mean a broad and inclusive range of elements. Even if they were once known as secondary antecedents, they have recently become rather critical as a result of technological advances.

- **Physical context.** Any element that contributes to the designing of the physical environment where interactions take place relates to this variable. Over the years, this category has attracted the attention of many marketing and architecture academics. Places are not only spaces for exchange, but they are also part of experiential contents as the cases of so-called starchitects and their striking buildings: the Guggenheim Museum, the MAXXI Roma by Zaha Hadid, and the Louvre Abu Dhabi by Jean Nouvel are just a few excellent examples.
- **Digital environment.** Digital platforms also greatly contribute to audience engagement by stimulating and supporting people in their interactions but despite their practical relevance, they are still largely understudied. Digital platforms refer both to the interaction between brand and individual and to the interaction among visitors. Online participation has relevant social aspects, which largely contribute to creating value while digital environments turn co-creation into a concrete opportunity for many (Conner 2013). Establishing a network of relationships is a key driver of value creation, and technologies offer visitors the opportunities to interact, debate, and discuss. Art content becomes the initial stimulus visitors interact with to create unity. Social media, in particular, connects museums with their audiences, thus creating a participatory experience, an effect that has emerged even more intensely during the recent Covid pandemic. Especially anticipated experiences benefit from digital technologies. Several kinds of digital content are possible, such as portals, virtual tours,

and online exhibits, e-learning resources, online collections, and digital archives and libraries.

- **Social environment.** Social stimuli are very effective in generating audience engagement. Cultural experiences become vehicles for the attribution of social signs and meanings. The latter represents the 'glue' of a specific target or community, and the driver of audience engagement for any individual within that community (McAlexander et al. 2002). Sharing is a critical antecedent of audience engagement because tastes and preferences for artistic offerings are often transferred to others.

2.3 Leverage the Drivers of Audience Engagement and the Role of Museum Cultural Mediation

The above three categories of audience engagement taken together build an overall framework that is useful for museums in designing their cultural experiences (Figure 2.1). The latter should comply with two key principles, common in marketing management:

1 The visitor experience must be specifically designed to reach a specific target. Every visitor's segment needs a specific experience which is specifically designed. Although individual characteristics are not manageable, they still drive brand targeting, communication, and customer interactions. Thus, an analysis of them is fundamental both for segmentation and for the design of the visitor experience.

2 The visitor experience must be consistently designed to tell a compelling story. Museums, especially, face a specific and significant challenge: the extreme fragmentation of their collections. Over time, museums create their unique heritage by collecting pieces and artifacts that are by nature disjointed fragments. Thanks to the consistent use of drivers, museums can tell new and unifying stories able "to engage visitors' attention and to help them appreciate, understand and make sense of what they are looking at" (Lwin 2012, p. 227). Drivers need to be used as parts of a consistent framework, reducing – and even hopefully eliminating – any contradictory stimuli for visitors.

Whenever the story is by definition challenging, museum cultural mediation might act as a key tool to make the story understandable for visitors. However, to leverage this element of their offering, museums must do much more than simply launch a programme. As there is

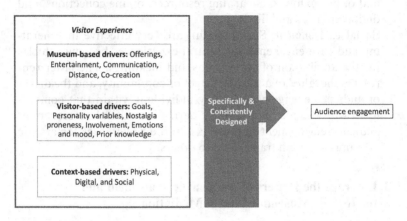

Figure 2.1 Audience engagement: drivers.
Source: Our elaboration.

no "one best solution" when it comes to visitor experiences, museum cultural mediation can achieve success (i.e. increasing audience engagement) only if it is differentiated according to the visitor targets, and included in global and consistent positioning. These topics will be further addressed in the next sections of this book.

References

Addis, M. (2005). New technologies and cultural consumption. Edutainment is born! *European Journal of Marketing*, *39*(7/8), 729–736.

Addis, M. (2020). *Engaging Brands*. Taylor & Francis – Routledge: London.

Addis, M., and Holbrook, M. B. (2001). On the conceptual link between mass customisation and experiential consumption: An explosion of subjectivity. *Journal of Consumer Behaviour: An International Research Review*, *1*(1), 50–66.

Addis, M., and Rurale, A. (2020). A call to revise cultural business management. In M. Addis and A. Rurale (Eds.), *Managing the Cultural Business* (pp. 1–31). Taylor & Francis – Routledge: London.

American Alliance of Museums (2020). "The American alliance of museums urges US Congress to include $4 billion for nonprofit museums in COVID-19 economic relief legislation." Accessed on May 13, 2021. Available at https://www.aam-us.org/2020/03/19/american-alliance-of-museums-urges-us-congress-   to-include-4-billion-for-nonprofit-museums-in-COVID-19-economic-relief-legislation/.

Barab, S. (2006). Design-based research. In R. K. Sawyer (Ed.), *Cambridge Handbook of the Learning Sciences* (pp. 151–170). Cambridge University Press: Cambridge.

Black, G. (2005). *The Engaging Museum: Developing Museums for Visitor Involvement*. Taylor & Francis – Routledge: London.

Brodie, R. J., Hollebeek, L. D., Jurić, B., and Ilić, A. (2011). Customer engagement: Conceptual domain, fundamental propositions, and implications for research. *Journal of Service Research*, *14*(3), 252–271.

Carnwath, J. D., and Brown, A. S. (2014). *Understanding the Value and Impacts of Cultural Experiences: A Literature Review*. Arts Council England: London.

Carù, A., and Cuadrado-García, M. (2020). Understanding the arts customer: The mistake of overlooking customer experience. In M. Addis and A. Rurale (Eds.), *Managing the Cultural Business* (pp. 213–243). Taylor & Francis – Routledge: London.

Colbert, F., and St-James, Y. (2014). Research in arts marketing: Evolution and future directions. *Psychology & Marketing*, *31*(8), 566–575.

Conner, L. (2013). *Audience Engagement and the Role of Arts Talk in the Digital Era*. Palgrave Macmillan: New York.

Doyle, J. (2013). *Hold it Against Me: Difficulty and Emotion in Contemporary Art*. Duke University Press: Durham, NC.

Falk, J. H., and Dierking, L. D. (2016). *The museum Experience Revisited*. Taylor & Francis – Routledge: London.

Goulding, C. (2000). The museum environment and the visitor experience. *European Journal of Marketing*, *34*(3–4), 261–278.

Hennig-Thurau, T., and Houston, M. B. (2019). *Entertainment Science. Data Analytics and Practical Theory for Movies, Games, Books, and Music*. Springer Nature: Cham.

Holbrook, M. B., and Hirschman, E. C. (1982). The experiential aspects of consumption: Consumer fantasies, feelings, and fun. *Journal of Consumer Research*, *9*(2), 132–140.

Hollebeek, L. D. (2011). Exploring customer brand engagement: Definition and themes. *Journal of Strategic Marketing*, *19*(7), 555–573.

ICOM (2020). "Museums and Covid-19: 8 steps to support community resilience." Accessed on April 29, 2021. Available at https://icom.museum/en/news/museums-and-COVID-19-8-steps-to-support-community-resilience/.

Kemp, E. (2015). Engaging consumers in aesthetic offerings: Conceptualizing and developing a measure for arts engagement. *International Journal of Nonprofit and Voluntary Sector Marketing*, *20*(2), 137–148.

Lemon, K. N., and Verhoef, P. C. (2016). Understanding customer experience throughout the customer journey. *Journal of Marketing*, *80*(6), 69–96.

Lwin, S. M. (2012). Whose stuff is it? A museum storyteller's strategies to engage her audience. *Narrative Inquiry*, *22*(2), 226–246.

McAlexander, J. H., Schouten, J. W., and Koenig, H. F. (2002). Building brand community. *Journal of Marketing*, *66*(1), 38–54.

Mujtaba, T., Lawrence, M., Oliver, M., and Reiss, M. J. (2018). Learning and engagement through natural history museums. *Studies in Science Education*, *54*(1), 41–67.

NEMO (2020). *Survey on the Impact of the COVID-19 Situation on Museums in Europe*. Accessed on May 8, 2022. Available at: https://www.nemo.org/

fileadmin/Dateien/public/NEMO_documents/NEMO_Corona_Survey_Results_6_4_20.pdf.

NEMO (2021). "Follow-up Survey on the Impact of the COVID-19 Pandemic on Museums in Europe. Final Report." Accessed on June 23, 2022. Available at: https://www.ne-mo.org/fileadmin/Dateien/public/NEMO_documents/NEMO_COVID19_FollowUpReport_11.1.2021.pdf.

Shaw, G., and Williams, A. (2009). Knowledge transfer and management in tourism organizations: An emerging research agenda. *Tourism Management*, *30*(3), 325–335.

Sørensen, F., and Jensen, J. F. (2015). Value creation and knowledge development in tourism experience encounters. *Tourism Management*, 46, 336–346.

Stern, B. B. (1992). Historical and personal nostalgia in advertising text: The fin de siècle effect. *Journal of Advertising*, *21*(4), 11–22.

Styvén, M. E. (2010). The need to touch: Exploring the link between music involvement and tangibility preference. *Journal of Business Research*, *63*(9–10), 1088–1094.

UNESCO (2020). "Museums Facing COVID-19 Challenges Remain Engaged with Communities." Accessed on May 1, 2022. Available at: https://en.unesco.org/news/museums-facing-COVID-19-challenges-remain-engaged-communities.

Venkatesh, A. L., and Meamber, L. A. (2006). Arts and aesthetics: Marketing and cultural production. *Marketing Theory*, *6*(1), 11–39.

Weil, S. E. (1997). The museum and the public. *Museum Management and Curatorship*, *16*(3), 257–271.

Wood, E., and Wolf, B. (2008). Between the lines of engagement in museums: Indiana University and the Children's Museum of Indianapolis. *Journal of Museum Education*, *33*(2), 121–130.

Zaichkowsky, J. L. (1994). The personal involvement inventory: Reduction, revision, and application to advertising. *Journal of Advertising*, *23*(4), 59–70.

3 Museum Cultural Mediation
From Competences to Best Practices

Zoe Giannotti

3.1 The Increasing Relevance of Museum Cultural Mediation in Cultural Experiences

Arts organizations are becoming experience-centred institutions (Kotler et al. 2008), and emotions, in particular, play an important role in this (Holbrook and Hirschman 1982). Despite this widely established consideration, 'one best solution' does not exist when it comes to visitor experiences, but this approach is intrinsically liked to the role of the museum cultural mediator. The need for this role arises from the recent revolutionary challenges museums have faced in communication, with dissolving traditional audience groups in societies with no borders. A new culture of learning appropriate to time is required and cultural mediation needs to develop accordingly (Mörsch and Chrusciel 2012). The latter must reflect customers' interactive needs in order to engage visitors in compelling experiences. Experiences result from a journey that can be traced back to four phases (Lusch and Vargo 2010): the pre-experience phase, in which the consumer anticipates, dreams, imagines, and plans what will experience next; the purchase phase, when consumers buy the experience; the central phase of the experience, when consumers interact with the product; and the experience of remembrance, in which the consumer re-lives past experiences through memories and stories. Since customers often prefer artistic offerings that include active participation, interaction and, if possible, co-creation (Styvén 2010), the resulting engagement encourages museums to customize their experiences according to visitors' specific needs (Falk and Dierking 2016). To reach this goal, the museum cultural mediator can establish intimate bonds that culminate in enduring relational exchanges between producers and customers, which can affect both loyalty and pleasure (Sashi 2012). Therefore, the challenge for cultural institutions is to shift from a traditional, so-called one-way

DOI: 10.4324/9781003352754-3

communicative approach to a more modern, two-way communication approach, in which interaction and feedback are continuous (Kumar and Gupta 2016). To achieve this, museums must develop ongoing conversations with their audience (Venkatesan 2017).

The traditional guided tour is no longer able to satisfy the demands of an evolving public, eager to learn but also to be questioned and listened to (Varnum and Grossmann 2017). Generally, museums rely on traditional communication tools, such as captions, panels, multimedia content, catalogues, publications, and audio guides. However, they cannot replace the engaging power of direct connections, which is fundamental for established and effective personal relationships (Prabavathi and Nagasubramani 2018). In terms of content, the communication of cultural institutions is often strongly focused on their pieces of art, highlighting their artistic value within specialist communities. Such an approach may threaten the inclusivity of the experience, targeting it only to regular visitors, thereby neglecting the needs of many other groups that appreciate the museums' offerings for various aspects beyond their aesthetic value (Kliuchko 2020). Communication in designing engaging cultural experiences is especially crucial, and museum cultural mediation can represent a powerful tool for visitors to improve their approach to the cultural experience. This is the main difference from the traditional guided tour: museum cultural mediation adapts style to the specific audience and facilitates dialogue, turning attention, interest, and involvement into conversation (Miniero and Holst 2020). Thus, it stimulates the visitor's active participation, encouraging dynamic and co-creative cultural experiences (Bulatova et al. 2020). Towards that goal, museums have to help visitors to play with and ultimately overcome their limits and fears in proactive exchanges with the surrounding environment. Visitor expectations and demands rely on engaging communication, where they are not only the recipients of information but also actively and appreciatively involved players, where, as mentioned, they are not only spoken to but also listened to (Miniero and Holst 2020).

Finding ways to increase customer engagement has emerged as a top priority for any artistic or cultural organization (Addis and Rurale 2020), which needs to adopt a customer-based strategy (Falk 2009; Falk and Dierking 2016). To that end, designing memorable experiences is the key:

> On one hand cultural institutions should try to work on a content that integrates both emotions and information if their goal is to foster engagement; on the other hand, pure emotional content

might work if the goal of the communication is to leverage on engagement and attachment between the institutions and the public.

(Miniero and Holst 2020: 318)

3.2 Museum Cultural Mediation: The Current Situation

The first museums were established almost half a millennium ago, while 90%–95% of the world's museums have been created since the end of the Second World War (Boylan 2013). This soaring growth in number, range, variety, and richness is in line with similar developments in museum employment: "From just two traditional types of employees, the scholar-curators and the non-professional support workers (technical, maintenance, and security personnel), the museum workforce now includes an almost bewildering range of positions and job titles" (Boylan 2013: 9).

Mediation arose from this scenario, as a new practical form of free and dynamic dialogues with the public within exhibition spaces: any type of art and museum can benefit from it, as long as an innovative and personal approach is adopted to customize the experience and immerse the consumer in the visit. The concept of immersion has long been used in the field of arts and culture (Duhaime et al. 1995), often concerning an extraordinary experience where "what we feel, what we wish and what we think are in harmony" (Csikszentmihalyi 1997: 29). Carù and Cova (2003) highlight that enjoyment results from a progressive cognitive conquest of audiences that requires their knowledge capital. Since customers act as co-creators of their own experience (Peñaloza et al. 2012), understanding their visitor-based drivers of engagement (goals, personality features, nostalgia proneness, involvement, emotions and mood, and prior knowledge) is especially relevant for museum managers. Only engaged customers might be willing to share their knowledge and participate in activities and new experiences (Yachin 2018).

This might be especially challenging for contemporary art museums, which often convey high levels of perceived difficulty (Doyle 2013), thus generating common communication gaps (Bulatova et al. 2020). The communication gap in question emerges from the recipient's lack of understanding of the "coded message", i.e. the meaning of the work proposed by the artist is often by definition quite complex. In these cases, cultural mediators mediate relationships through collective dialogues, supporting the communicative process (Rappoport

2017). Since interactive experiences commonly drive customer engagement (Van Doorn et al. 2010), co-creation should be guaranteed (Addis 2020). Visitors whose cognitive process is stimulated often return (Bulatova et al. 2020). They no longer expect to receive complete explanations but instead want to be part of a creative process. Mediators are conductors of communication, focusing more on visitors and their experiences and feelings than on the works of art and their contents. Internal elaboration and cognition are thus stimulated through explanations, empathy, and immersion (Bulatova et al. 2020). Museum cultural mediators listen more than speak, enabling the visitor's 'emancipation'.

This is challenging for many museums: "Despite this widely established consideration, cultural institutions cannot often adopt a customer experience-oriented approach consistent with the peculiarities of the contexts in which they operate" (Carù and Cuadrado 2020: 215). Nowadays, despite the increasing relevance of the experience-oriented approach, little is known about the necessary skills of the museum cultural mediator and their adoption worldwide. The following empirical analyses, run by way of benchmarking, aim to fill this gap.

3.3 Museum Cultural Mediation in Educational Programmes

To identify the skills needed for museum cultural mediation, a benchmarking analysis has been run. Benchmarking is a technique that dates back to the late seventies and allows for the carrying out of a qualitative and quantitative analysis, aimed at highlighting the strengths and weaknesses of current and potential competitors. It is, therefore, a systematic and continuous process to compare one's efficiency in terms of productivity, quality, and practice with those companies and organizations that represent excellence (Karlof and Ostblom 1993). The selected educational programmes were chosen according to the following criteria:

* The European educational programmes were taught in Italian, English, French, Spanish, or German.
* The educational programmes were aimed at training the museum cultural mediator.
* Complete information regarding the courses of study was available on the official websites of the academies and universities.
* The courses analysed were delivered in the 2020–2021 academic year. As a result, 33 educational programmes run in 2021 were

included in the benchmarking analysis, covering Italy, France, Spain, Belgium, Germany, Switzerland, Canada, and the UK. Table 3.1 presents the complete list of the analysed educational programmes.

Table 3.1 The educational programmes in the benchmarking

Educational institution	Educational program	City, Country
Albertina Academy of Fine Arts, Turin	Communication and enhancement of contemporary artistic heritage	Turin, Italy
Albertina Academy of Fine Arts, Turin	Art teaching	Turin, Italy
Academy of Fine Arts of Bologna	Didactics of Art and Cultural Mediation for artistic heritage	Bologna, Italy
Brera Academy of Fine Arts	Communication and teaching of contemporary art	Milan, Italy
Brescia Academy of Fine Arts Santa Giulia	Communication and teaching of art	Brescia, Italy
Academy of Fine Arts of Catania	Art teaching and cultural mediation	Catania, Italy
Florence Academy of Fine Arts	Didactics for museums	Florence, Italy
Florence Academy of Fine Arts	Art teaching	Florence, Italy
Naples Academy of Fine Arts	Didactics and cultural mediation of heritage	Naples, Italy
Academy of Fine Arts of Palermo	Art teaching and cultural mediation of artistic heritage	Palermo, Italy
Academy of Fine Arts of Palermo	Art teaching and cultural mediation of artistic heritage	Palermo, Italy
Academy of Fine Arts in Rome	Communication and enhancement of contemporary artistic heritage	Rome, Italy
Academy of Fine Arts in Rome	Communication and teaching of the museum and exhibition events	Rome, Italy
Academy of Fine Arts of Verona	Workshop management" – cultural mediation of art	Verona, Italy
Aix-Marseille Université	Cultural mediation of the arts	Aix-Marseille, France
Birkbeck University of London	Museum Cultures	London, UK

(*Continued*)

Educational institution	Educational program	City, Country
Ecole Eac	Cultural mediation and communication	Paris–Lyon, France
Education University of Karlsruhe	Cultural mediation	Karlsruhe, Germany
Goldsmiths University of London	The Arts and Learning	London, UK
Goethe University of Frankfurt am Main	Art, media, cultural education	Frankfurt am Main, Germany
Institut Catholique de Toulouse	Mediation and management of cultural actions	Toulouse, France
Koninklijke Academie voor Schoone Kunsten van Antwerpen	Educational Master's in Visual Arts	Antwerp, Belgium
University of Murcia	Education and Museums, Heritage, Identity and Cultural Mediation	Murcia, Spain
University of Ferrara	Didactics, education and mediation in museums and cultural heritage	Ferrara, Italy
Sant'Orsola Benincasa University	Museum educator	Naples, Italy
University of Bologna	Visual arts	Bologna, Italy
University of Cassino	Advanced training course in heritage education and museum communication	Cassino, Italy
Catholic University of Milan	Educational services for the artistic heritage of museums and visual arts	Milan, Italy
Roma Tre University	Advanced museum education studies	Rome, Italy
University of Barcelona	Contemporary Art	Barcelona, Spain
Universitè de Neuchatel	Museum studies	Neuchatel, Swiss
University of Manchester	Arts Management, Policy, and Practice	Manchester, UK
Zurich University of the Arts	Art pedagogy	Zurich, Swiss

Source: our elaboration.

Skills were analysed by measuring the European Credit Transfer and Accumulation System (ECTS) number which states the workload required of students, as communicated on their institution's official websites. The ECTSs were then tallied for the four skill areas resulting from the educational programmes. Each programme attributes a higher ECTS number to one of the four areas. The four skill areas used in the analysis are as follows:

Historical and Artistic Skills. This skill set refers to the theory and practice of art, including courses and activities such as History of Art, Art Criticism, Phenomenology, and Aesthetics. Together they build the theoretical basis for cultural mediation providing the proper knowledge to approach, understand, contextualize, and analyse the work of art towards the development of critical thinking. In this sense, Historical-Artistic Skills define the foundations of museum cultural mediation, which focuses on one-way communication of artistic heritage knowledge. There is little space for the co-creative visitor in these programmes. An example of a significant educational programme is *"Mediation Culturelle des arts"* at Aix-Marseille University, France. In this educational programme, several high-quality courses are taught, such as "Aesthetics and cultural practices" (9 ECTSs), "Theory and discourses on art" (9 ECTSs) "Cultural planning and knowledge of the professional field" (6 ECTSs), and "Transversal art and themes" (3 ECTSs).

Education and Communication Skills. The second area refers to communication in a broad sense. It includes courses such as Pedagogy, Communication, Sociology, Anthropology, and Psychology which all share the commitment to develop skills for effective communication, fundamental for museum cultural mediation. Education and Communication Skills support mediators in teaching and expanding their interactive and dynamic activities to build a 'bridge' between art and the public. These kinds of skill support museums in engaging their visitors during the cultural experiences by stimulating the visitor's reflections and emotional response through the search for active communication and co-creative experiences. A good example is *"Educacion y Museos, Patrimonio, Identidad y Mediacion Cultural"* at the University of Murcia, Spain. This educational programme aims to provide students with a comprehensive vision of the museum as a social and cultural ecosystem by way of courses such as "Learning in museums" (6 ECTSs), "Communication and dissemination strategies" (6 ECTSs), "Visitor studies" (3 ECTSs), and "Social inclusion strategies in museums" (6 ECTSs).

Museography and Design Skills. This area focuses on the design, implementation, and communication of cultural experiences. This kind of skill is developed by a wide range of courses including Museography, Museology, Organization of Media Art, and so on, which investigate new tools and techniques for supporting cultural offerings and defining a vision for museums. Indeed, students enrolled in these courses learn how to use museums as interactive platforms capable of satisfying visitor needs. Thus, according to these skills, cultural mediation facilitates the understanding of the works of art and their presentation through a thorough dialogue with the environment. An example of that is the program entitled "*Museum Cultures*" at Birkbeck University of London. This educational programme aims to develop a broad range of key theoretical and practical skills from critical thinking and writing to a ten-week supervised work placement in museums, galleries, and archives. Other courses include "Museum Cultures – Approaches, Problems, and Competences" (30 ECTSs), "Curatorship as a critical practice" (15 ECTSs), and "Curating difficult stories: museums, exhibitions and activism in art" (15 ECTSs).

Legal and Economic Skills. This last set of skills deals with the strategies for conveying messages to different audience targets, including time planning, sustainability, and social impact. The analysed educational programmes focus on economics, management, and law. These skills relate to a view of museum cultural mediation that supports the idea of 'inhabiting' the museum is in line with external changes and is embedded in online and offline global environments. A good example of the interest that exists in this category of skills is the "Cultural mediation and communication" programme at the Ecole Eac in Paris and Lyon, France. In this programme, 70% of the ECTSs focuses on the knowledge of the professional environment and its practices, by understanding diverse kinds of art, learning about the management of core activities and how to stimulate interaction with audiences, and acquiring good practices to foster the promotion of arts and artists with all audiences. The acquisition of 78 ECTSs in project management is a distinctive feature of this programme.

Besides the differences in the four areas of skills, the analysed education programmes share two aspects:

* A strong focus on the planning and management of cultural mediation.
* A strong focus on the revitalization and questioning of the traditional use of the artwork and the interpretation of museums as a medium.

Having broached the subject of the skills needed for museum cultural mediation, an analysis of best practices can be conducted to complete our understanding of the current state of museum cultural mediation.

3.4 Museum Cultural Mediation in Museums around the World

Skills developed during educational programmes are then applied in practical policies around the world. To investigate how this professional experience is designed and identify the best cases that have been established in ongoing practices, we ran a second benchmarking analysis on a selected sample of museums. The selected museums were chosen according to the following criteria:

- National and international museums of modern and contemporary art that list museum cultural mediation among its educational services.
- Clear statement on the official website on the cultural mediation experience offered to visitors.
- Continual, active use of museum cultural mediation between January 2020 and August 2022.
- The availability of information in Italian, English, French, Spanish, and German. As a result, a final sample of 68 museums were included in the benchmarking analysis. Table 3.2 presents the complete list of the analysed museums.

Table 3.2 The analysed museums

Museums
Bonnefantenmuseum of Maastricht
Casteel of Rivoli of Tourin
Centre d'Art La Panera of Lleida
Centre Pompidou of Paris
Centro de Arte Dos Mayo of Madrid
Lisbon Modern Art Centre
Luigi Pecci Centre for Contemporary Art
Bramante Cloister of Rome
Cobra museum in Amstelveen
Venice Biennale Foundation
Venice Foundation - House of the Three Oci
Palazzo Strozzi Foundation in Florence
Pinault Foundation (Palazzo Grassi - Punta della Dogana) of Venice
PRADA Foundation of Milan
Sandretto King of Turin Foundation
Borghese Gallery in Rome
Uffizi Gallery of Florence
Galleries of Italy, Vicenza, Palazzo Leoni Montanari
National Gallery of Modern and Contemporary Art
GAMeC of Bergamo

(Continued)

Museums

"Garage" Museum of Modern Art in Moscow
Het Nieuwe Institut in Rotterdam
Irish Museum of Modern Art, Dublin
KW Berlin
Latvian Centre for Contemporary Art (LCCA)
Mambo of Bologna
MACRO of Rome
MAN of Nuoro
Mart of Train and Rovereto
Maxxi of Rome
MOMA of New York
Mudec in Milan
Mumok of Vienna
Bargello Museums of Florence
Barcelona Museum of Contemporary Art
Museo Berardo in Lisbona
Terragona Museum of Modern Art
Museum of Modern and Contemporary Art of Trento and Rovereto
Museum of Contemporary Art of Castilla Y Leon
Museum of Latino American art of Buenos Aires
Museum of the Twentieth Century Milan
Budapest Museum of Fine Arts
Museum of Rome - Palazzo Braschi
Museo Galileo - Institute and Museum of the History of Science in Florence
Ludwig Museum in Budapest
Madre Museum of Naples
Marino Marini Museum in Florence
Reina Sofia National Art Museum in Madrid
Novecento Museum Florence
Antwerp Museum of Contemporary Art
Poldi Pezzoli Museum, Milan
National Art Museum of Ukraine
National Centre for Contemporary Arts in Russia
Palace of Exhibitions in Rome
Peggy Guggenheim of Venezia
Brera Picture Gallery
Rijksmuseum di Amsterdam
Russian Museum
Russian State Exhibition and art centre
Scottish National Gallery of Modern Art
SMAK of Ghent
State Hermitage Museum in Russia
London Tate
Milan Triennale
Van Abbemuseum in Eindhoven
Vleeshal for Contemporary Art in Middelburg
Wiels of Forest in Bruxelles

Source: our elaboration.

The analysis was conducted according to the model developed by Wimmer (2010), which sets the quality of cultural mediation in a specific market segment (namely, music) that could be easily extended to other segments. Indeed, as Fuchs (2010) states "the quality attribution process is a normative process that depends on individual and social values" (p. 183), the growing differentiation of cultural mediation is developed through quality debates. Wimmer's model presents three mediation quality areas as follows:

- **Structural quality.** This concerns, among other things, collaboration and communication policies within the institution, financing, project management, and partnerships with cultural and training institutions. This area focuses especially on: *communication* (i.e. the transparency of information), *organization* (i.e. the organizational structure of experiences), and *management of partnerships*, which is the existence of collaboration with other organizations.
- **Process quality.** This refers to the artistic and pedagogical concept as well as the possibilities of participation for the public and participants; within the process, quality is studied. The area refers especially to: *collaboration with mediators* which concerns the relationship between museum-mediators; and the *organizational quality of projects* which concerns the existence of differentiated offerings and an experiential or educational approach.
- **Quality of the product.** This concerns the artistic and pedagogical implementation of mediation, in line with the objectives set by the institution. Specifically, it encompasses the area of Wimmer's product quality (2010) which develops in these two areas of relevance: *systems of contact with the public* that regards the interaction with customers and good performance in the long term; and *other figures present* which concerns the space of the mediator and this figure's boundaries as foreseen by the museum structure.

Information on the three areas was gathered through the analysis of these museums' websites. Specifically, each area has been analysed by getting data on a few specific variables. Table 3.3 presents the list of variables that operationalize each area, with its best cases.

An analysis of each museum policy according to the three areas of quality allows for the identification of a few best cases that represent reference points for other institutions that aim to improve their performances.

With specific regard to *structural quality,* a significant application is the one made by the Irish Museum of Modern Art of Dublin

Table 3.3 Analysis of mediation quality

Area of cultural mediation quality	Variables	Best cases
Structural quality	The level of transparency, clarity and completeness of the information presented (Does the site provide clear information? Does it clarify what the objective of the proposed mediation service is? What is the average duration of the visit? Is a reservation required?)	Irish Museum of Modern Art of Dublin; Museum of Modern Art of Barcelona
Process quality	The level of heterogeneity, customization, and partnership of the proposed activities (Is mediation a single service or are there different types of activities proposed? Who do these activities target? Do they involve collaborations with associations or training institutes?)	Reina Sofia National Art Museum in Madrid; K W Berlin
Quality of the product	The level of synergies with other communication and educational roles, policies and tools (guided tours, audio guides) The level of possible interaction and contact between museums and their audiences (feedback systems, touch-points, customer experience reports, ...)	K W Berlin

Source: our elaboration.

and the Museum of Modern Art of Barcelona. These best cases are notable because of the absolute clarity of the information conveyed through their websites. In the case of the Irish Museum of Modern Art of Dublin, the mediator, who is called the 'visitor engagement operator', is available in two versions. The first is an actively present, defined professional role located in the rooms of the museum. The visitor engagement operators offer their services to anyone without any need for a reservation, and with no limits in reference to the number of customers. The second version is organized on the basis of a previous booking, has a limit of 20 people, and is designed to last for 30 minutes. Further, in this museum, cultural mediation relies on a wide network of players: activities are developed with industry professionals and artists deliberately chosen to increase participation and interaction. Educational projects are launched in collaboration with public and private institutions that deal with education, artistic, and social production. The Museum of Modern Art of Barcelona also offers two kinds of museum cultural mediation, but they are different in terms of their level of customization. The basic experience proposes a list of themes which the visitor can choose from on-site, and artists, researchers, curators, and professionals can then act as mediators. For this experience, booking is mandatory, there is no limit in terms of the number of visitors and it lasts one hour. The second experience is customized, reservations are mandatory, it sets limits of a minimum of 15 and a maximum of 30 people and lasts 1.5 hours.

Regarding *process quality,* an important example is that of the Reina Sofia National Art Museum in Madrid and the K W Berlin. Their significant investments in terms of communication, content, and education make these cases interesting references. The museum cultural mediator proactively seeks to engage all segments of visitors, communicating the vision of the museum, and providing information on artists and exhibitions, both individually and collectively. The cultural mediation projects are heterogeneous and seek to focus attention on specific issues that are considered of interest to the wider public. Moreover, artists are commonly invited to hold workshops such as dance, performance, and drawing while professionals from the industry are involved in conferences and publicity events. Both paid contracts and curricular internships are offered, and in the case of the Reina Sofia National Art Museum in Madrid, mediators work with the Engagement and Learning team to prepare the materials and resources needed both for scheduling events and for providing accurate feedback on the visitor experience.

Regarding *the quality of the product,* K W Berlin provides a vital model. This best case is particularly relevant, as few of the study subjects produce an annual report covering all museum reports including that of the museum cultural mediator. Furthermore, a specific section on the site is reserved for this figure, which therefore provides balance regarding information on the services offered.

3.5 A Typology of Museum Cultural Mediation

The wide variety of existing educational programmes pushes museums to adopt heterogeneous museum cultural mediation experiences: since skill sets differ greatly, and they drive the positioning of museum cultural mediation, experiences are consequently very different, not only with respect to the three quality areas of Wimmer's model (2010). For instance, they vary in the first point of contact and interaction, in the promotion and the networks of partnerships with associations and experts, in their level of communication clarity about goals, knowledge and the role of visitors, in their feedback processes, in their long-term performance, in the activities offered for specific targets, and so on. Although these differences might be relevant, such a high level of heterogeneity can be summarized in four different categories of museum cultural mediation, with different levels of communication:

1. **Highly Structured Mediation.** This category includes all the museums offering defined and differentiated mediation experiences. Specifically, these cases mostly present the information on their websites with great clarity. In almost all cases, they have collaborations with associations or training institutes to develop different projects or activities that involve mediation on or off-site. Very often they are directed at 'specific' target audiences, in particular, teenage audiences, children, people with disabilities as well as families. These museums frequently promote mediation experiences on their website by way of a specific section (commonly education).

2. **Structured Mediation.** This second category includes museums that are mostly geared towards specific targets, such as families, primary schools, people with disabilities, and so on. In general, this kind of museum offers visitors the opportunity to choose from a wide range of potential experiences in line with their preferences. These museums frequently present museum cultural mediation as an 'educational activity' in the teaching section of their websites, describing their activities with complete information and examples. As a result, finding information on museum cultural mediation is not always immediate. As with the highly structured mediation cases, these museums design their cultural mediation experiences in collaboration with artists, experts, public institutions (such as universities or academies), cultural associations, and so forth that are highly competent in educational services or in developing a relationship with the most fragile audiences. To sum up, this category of museums targets the general public with an inclusive approach, aiming to satisfy multiple visitors' needs simultaneously.

3. **Unstructured Mediation.** The third category includes museums that offer museum cultural mediation but only in a poorly defined and designed manner. Therefore, this kind of experience appears to be virtually the same as guided tours because they both aim to reach the same goal: educating the audience. The websites do not

contain a specific section focusing on mediation, which is instead commonly found in the 'guided tour' section. Consequently, communication regarding museum cultural mediation is confusing and incomplete.

4. **Absent Mediation.** The final category groups together museums that claim availability of museum cultural mediation but do not provide any information.

Empirical analysis made it possible to understand the purpose of museum cultural mediation, by highlighting the synergies between the areas of skill and quality according to Wimmer's model (2010). The wide range of potential skills and experiences stimulates a high differentiation of museum cultural mediation towards improvements in visitor value. To that end, communication is crucial. Indeed, highly structured mediation adopts active communication with visitors, by also stimulating interactions among visitors to make visits ever more engaging and dynamic experiences, and stimulates visitors' reflections and emotional responses, to reach engagement and attachment between the institutions and the public (Miniero and Holst 2020). Similarly, but to a lesser extent, structured mediation designs experiences that satisfy several needs at the same time, albeit by way of more traditional educational experiences. In this case, *historical and artistic* skills are crucial. In addition, unstructured mediation typically leverages both historical and artistic skills and education and communication skills to investigate which kind of communication works best with their target audience.

Since the experience in a museum is (and will always be) affected by environmental changes, it is fundamental to adapt to new trends to achieve success. Nowadays, the challenge for museums is to approach audiences in customized and highly tailored ways, to establish free and dynamic dialogue in order to produce empathy and emotions.

Museum cultural mediators could contribute greatly to this end but museums must know their audiences deeply: this is an essential ingredient of successful communication strategies to engage them effectively (Miniero and Holst 2020). An analysis of visitor value is the starting point of every such engaging experience.

References

Addis, M. (2020). *Engaging Brands.* Taylor & Francis – Routledge: London.

Addis, M., and Rurale, A. (2020). A call to revise cultural business management. In M. Addis and A. Rurale (Eds.), *Managing the Cultural Business* (pp. 1–31). Taylor & Francis – Routledge: London.

Boylan, P. (2013). *Museums: A Place to Work*. Taylor & Francis – Routledge: London.

Bulatova, A., Melnikova, S., and Zhuravleva, N. (2020). The significance of art mediation in bridging the communication gaps. *KnE Social Sciences*, *4*(2), 374–389.

Carù, A., and Cova, B. (2003). Revisiting consumption experience: A more humble but complete view of the concept. *Marketing Theory*, *3*(2), 267.

Carù, A., and Cuadrado-García, M. (2020). Understanding the arts customer: The mistake of overlooking customer experience. In M. Addis and A. Rurale (Eds.), *Managing the Cultural Business* (pp. 213–243). Taylor & Francis – Routledge: London.

Csikszentmihalyi, M. (1997). *Finding Flow*. Perseus: New York.

Doyle, J. (2013). *Hold It Against Me: Difficulty and Emotion in Contemporary Art*. Duke University Press: Durham, NC.

Duhaime, Joy, A., and Ross, C. (1995). Learning to "see": A folk phenomenology of the consumption of contemporary Canadian art. In J. F. Sherry, Jr. (Ed.), *Contemporary Marketing and Consumer Behavior: An Anthropological Sourcebook* (pp. 351–398). SAGE Publications: Thousand Oaks, CA.

Falk, J. (2009). *Identity and the Museum Visitor Experience*. Taylor & Francis – Routledge: London.

Falk, J. H., and Dierking, L. D. (2016). *The museum Experience Revisited*. Taylor & Francis – Routledge: London.

Fuchs, C. (2010). Alternative media as a critical media. *European Journal of Social Theory*, *13*(2), 173–192.

Holbrook, M. B., and Hirschman, E. C. (1982). The experiential aspects of consumption: Consumer fantasies, feelings, and fun. *Journal of Consumer Research*, *9*(2), 132–140.

Karloff, B., and Ostblom, S. (1993). *Benchmarking: A Signpost to Excellence in Quality and Productivity*. John Wiley & Sons: Hoboken, NJ.

Kotler, P., et al. (2008). *Museum Marketing and Strategy: Designing Missions, Building Audiences, Generating Revenue and Resources*. John Wiley & Sons: Hoboken, New Jersey.

Kliuchko, Y. (2020). Mediation in the context of the educational activity of the modern museum. *Culture and Arts in the Modern World*, *21*, 81–89.

Kumar, V., and Gupta, S. (2016). Conceptualizing the evolution and future of advertising. *Journal of Advertising*, *45*(3), 302–317.

Lusch, F., and Vargo, S. (2010). *S-D Logic: Accommodating, Integrating, Transdisciplinary*. University of Cambridge Press: Cambridge.

Miniero, G., and Holst, C. (2020). Corporate communication and the arts. In M. Addis, and A. Rurale (Eds.), *Managing the Cultural Business* (pp. 311–346). Taylor & Francis – Routledge: London.

Mörsch, C., and Chrusciel, A. (2012). *Time for Cultural Mediation*. Accessed on April 20, 2021. Available at: https://prohelvetia.ch/app/uploads/2017/09/tfcm_0_complete_publication.pdf

Peñaloza, L., Toulouse, N., and Visconti, L. (2012). Marketing management: A cultural perspective. In A. Carù, and B. Cova (Eds.), *Experiencing Consumption: Appropriating and Marketing Experiences* (pp. 164–177). Taylor & Francis – Routledge: London.

Prabavathi, R., and Nagasubramani, P. (2018). *Effective Oral and Written Communication.* Accessed on May 3, 2021. Available at: https://www. researchgate.net/publication/325087759_Effective_oral_and_written_ communication.

Rappoport, S. Kh. (2017). *From the Artist to the Viewer. Problems of Artistic Creativity.* Lan'; Planeta muzyki: St. Petersburg.

Sashi, C. (2012). Customer engagement, Buyer-Seller relationships, and social media. *Management Decision, 50*(2), 253–272.

Styvén, M. E. (2010). The need to touch: Exploring the link between music involvement and tangibility preference. *Journal of Business Research, 63*(9–10), 1088–1094.

Van Doorn, J., et al. (2010). Customer engagement behavior: Theoretical foundations and research directions. *Journal of Service Research, 13*(3), 253–266.

Varnum, M. E. W., and Grossmann, I. (2017). Cultural change: The how and the why. *Perspective on Psychological Science, 12*(5). Accessed on July 10, 2022. Available at: https://www.researchgate.net/publication/ 314037833_Cultural_Change_The_How_and_the_Why.

Venkatesan, R. (2017). Executing on a customer engagement strategy. *Journal of the Academy of Marketing Science, 45*(3), 289–293.

Wimmer, C. (2010). Exchange die Kunst, Musik zu vermitteln: Qualitäten in der Musikvermittlung und Konzertpädagogik. Accessed on April 14, 2021. Available at: http://www.miz.org/downloads/dokumente/569/2010_Studie-Die_Kunst-Musik-zu-vermitteln_Stiftung-Mozarteum-Salzburg.pdf

Yachin, J. M. (2018). The customer journey: Learning from customers in tourism experience encounters. *Tourism Management Perspectives, 28*, 201–210.

4 Understanding Visitor Value in Museum Cultural Mediation

Rosina Baldo and Anna Minici

4.1 Museum Cultural Mediation: The Visitor's Point of View

The construct of consumer value has a significant role in the competitive advantage and long-term success of a business and forms the basis of all marketing activities (Morar 2013). Research has shown that the most important factor in repurchase intentions is consumer value. Visitor value analysis is crucial for a comprehensive understanding of visitors' subjective preferences (Holbrook and Morris 1999), with related positive effects for the development of successful long-term museum cultural mediation experiences.

Morris Holbrook was a pioneer in the definition of value as a core element of a buyer's consumption. Holbrook's typology of values includes efficiency, excellence, status, esteem, play, aesthetics, ethics, and spirituality (Holbrook and Morris 1999). A more recent distinction proposes that values are by nature functional or emotional (Morar 2013). Whatever typology is adopted, scholars in consumer behaviour and marketing agree that values need to be decomposed in order to measure visitor value, which is composed of expected or perceived benefits and sacrifices to be made for the visitor (either tangible or intangible) (Tasci 2016). As visitor value drives individual preferences subjectively, it represents the main criterion to segment the market: each person differs in terms of specific needs, goals, and expectations, making it impossible to define a priori what 'good value' is.

Museum cultural mediation is no exception: visitor value analysis of museum cultural mediation is expected to identify the specific values that drive preferences, satisfaction, engagement, and any other attitudinal or behavioural visitor response. Thus, value analysis of visitors in the context of museum cultural mediation offers precious insights to segment the market and design successful and engaging visitor experiences.

DOI: 10.4324/9781003352754-4

'Market segmentation' means dividing consumers/audiences who manifest different needs and requirements into homogeneous and distinct groups (Colbert 2017). These are established using a segmentation model (Jerry 2019) where the choice of segmentation variables can be made through two distinct approaches, represented by: an *a priori* and *a posteriori* model (Arimond and Elfessi 2001). The *a priori* model uses a correlation between pre-established variables and purchasing behaviour. In this approach, the criteria for segmenting the market are decided at the beginning of the process and usually include socio-demographic (gender, age, income, qualifications, profession) and psychographic (lifestyle) variables. It does not always require market research as data can also be found using available sources (Green 1977). It is an easy, quick, and inexpensive method to carry out. However, these benefits are offset by limited effectiveness: the obtained segments are poorly defined, especially concerning purchasing behaviour and the articulation of needs. Therefore, it does not allow for the identification of 'latent segments' that are formed on the basis of variables other than the ones taken into consideration (Weinstein 2004). With the *a posteriori* model, market research is used to identify segments (and therefore segmentation variables) that cannot be defined as a priori (Budeva and Mullen 2014). This research aims to provide information on the characteristics of potential users (for example, in the case of a new product, it is possible to observe how desire and the intent to purchase change the profile of the interviewees). The advantages are numerous, including greater precision in segmentation and greater effectiveness in formulating marketing strategy and the offering formula. Obviously, in this case greater availability of time and resources is required (Weinstein 2004).

The main purpose of the analysis is the personalization of offerings, making the visitor an active part and co-creator of it (Reynolds and Olson 2001). To achieve this goal, value decomposition is essential to highlight even the emotional and symbolic meanings of museum cultural mediation for visitors.

The starting point is the identification of attributes from the visitor's point of view. The attributes are selected, elicited, classified, and scaled by way of appropriate procedures (Bernard 2017). These techniques derive from the classification of cultural domains and aim to distinguish objects based on their perceived similarities or differences, through benefits and values. This allows the museum to understand what visitors are expecting or desire and drives a value segmentation based on their different needs. This knowledge drives the competitive advantage for museums, which can rely on useful insights to expand

and amplify their offerings. The means-ends chain model supports museums in reaching this goal.

Specifically, the means-ends chain model support organizations in identifying consequences directly related to every type of consumption. Several studies have shown that to understand consumer behaviour in-depth, qualitative research designs are useful to better investigate how consumption decisions are made and underlying evaluation criteria (Nunkoo and Ramkissoon 2009). The means-ends chain highlights the connection between attributes of museum experiences, the consumer's expected consequences (benefits), and the value system that guides their behaviour:

Attributes. Attributes represent the basic elements directly perceivable and related to the product (Jooyeon and SooCheong 2013). They are divided into the material (as if materially perceivable by the consumer through the five senses and their cognitive ability) and immaterial (i.e. not directly perceivable or assessable).

Benefits. Benefits are the positive consequences related to the attributes of the experiences (Botschen et al. 1999). They can either be functional (i.e. related to the 'operational' functions for which an experience is purchased), psychological (when they impact the personal sphere of the individual and are manifested in terms of elements, stimuli and sensations that contribute to making the consumer feel comfortable or that achieve personal expectations), or sociological (i.e. benefits that through the use of the product allow the consumer to be identified within social groups or categories to which they aspire to belong) (Xiao and Guo 2018). Within the museum sector, 'operational' benefits relate to the primary goals of museums, such as carrying out research involving the tangible and intangible evidence of humanity and its environment, exhibiting it for the purposes of study after it has been acquired, preserved, and communicated (ICOM 2004). The psychological benefits relate to the restorative effects of the museum environment (such as escape and calm) on the psychological well-being of visitors. Finally, the sociological benefits include extrinsic effects that improve interpersonal skills – a museum visit may prove to be a way of strengthening one's social relationships or establishing new ones.

Values. Finally, values represent the overall goals of consumers' lives. They are divided into instrumental values that are the individual's preferred modes of behaviour (e.g., some individuals like to be seen as constantly in line with the times and for this reason, they *surround* themselves with items consistent with such criteria, such as clothes in line with current fashions, innovative technologies, etc.), and terminal values, which are the conditions of life that the individual aspires to achieve (De Oliveira Castro et al. 2018).

Thanks to the means-ends chain, it is possible to obtain a complete picture of visitor value and then segment the market, customize the offering, and finally design engaging museum cultural mediation experiences.

4.2 The Research Design for Exploring Visitor Value

This research aims to run the *a posteriori* segmentation for three reasons. First, museum cultural mediation is a new field with negligible studies, leaving much to be discovered. Second, understanding visitor value is a starting point for every marketing strategy. Third, this approach to the market offers the most precise, concrete, and safest results.

To analyse visitor value in museum cultural mediation, the semi-structured, in-depth qualitative interview method was adopted; it is one of the main methods of data collection used in qualitative research (Ritchie et al. 2003). Important studies have stressed the importance of talking to people to grasp their point of view (Burgess 2007). Indeed, language is crucial in social research since it illuminates the meaning and value proposition of the experience.

The in-depth interview is a qualitative research technique that involves conducting an intensive, individual interview with a few respondents to explore their perspectives on a particular idea, programme, or situation (Boyce and Neale 2006). This technique starts with a list of questions for the participants to decompose their visitor value. In this case, the questions focus on museum cultural mediation. The list of interview questions represents a sort of bridge between the objective of the research and the personal experience of the participants. In preparing the questions, two kinds of techniques were especially useful: projective and laddering techniques.

Projective techniques. Projective techniques support the researchers in connecting with the participants and represent an indirectly structured way of investigating the reasons underlying individual attitudes, behaviours, and preferences. They are not used to measure (which is the goal of quantitative methods, such as surveys) but to uncover feelings, beliefs, attitudes, and motivations that many consumers find difficult to articulate. Projective techniques help the researcher to enter the private worlds of participants to uncover their inner perspectives in a way they feel comfortable with (Donoghue 2000). They include four different techniques (Haire 1950): first, associative techniques based on word associations and metaphors; second, the completion techniques that ask for a sentence or story completion; third, the constructive techniques that are based on figure interpretations; and, finally, <u>the expressive techniques, which propose</u> third-person testing and role-playing.

Laddering techniques. Laddering is a useful technique in qualitative research to understand behaviours and is especially adopted in marketing to explore individuals' opinions, attitudes, and beliefs. It is highly recommended in research that treats customer value according to the models of Means-End Theory (Modesto et al. 2006). The respondent is asked about the kinds of characteristics that might describe or distinguish brands or products (in this case, experiences). This can be obtained in three ways (Perkins and Reynolds 1988): first, the technique entitled 'triadic sorting', where three distinct products or brands are presented, and the respondent is asked to indicate differences and similarities that two of them have with the third one (for instance, a typical question would be "In your opinion, what are the differences between museum cultural mediation and guided tours?"); the second technique is called 'preference-consumption differences', where the respondent is asked to indicate why a brand is more desirable compared to others (for instance, "In your opinion, what are the strengths and weaknesses of museum cultural mediation?"); and, finally, the last recommended technique is 'differences by occasion', where the customers are placed in a consumption scenario and asked to describe the features of this consumption (e.g. "Describe in your opinion what the ideal museum cultural mediation experience is"). Later in the interview, the questions proceed from product characteristics to user characteristics (Durgee 1986), which is associated with the second level of sequence attributes-consequences-values. The idea is to stimulate the respondents up a ladder of abstraction until they reach the level of values. For this purpose, repetitive and interactive questions are asked, first considering product attributes, second consequences of its use, and finally values.

These two techniques have been mainly used in preparing the list of questions for interviewing visitors involved in museum cultural mediation. The resulting list of 32 questions is structured into two sections:

1 Profiling questions, which address topics used to 'break the ice' and to understand the background of the participants.
2 Direct and indirect questions to gather information regarding the research question. The research question is quite basic and therefore crucial for segmenting the market: what is visitor value in the context of museum cultural mediation?

With museum cultural mediation being a relatively niche experience, we decided to focus on novice visitors. Thus, the research question was addressed with first-time customers of the museum cultural mediation experience. To recruit participants, three communication channels were used: a call for applications on social networks, personal contacts, and word of mouth in the researchers' network between June and July 2021. Instagram stories and posts explaining the required activity – that is, the museum cultural mediation experience and a subsequent interview concerning the experience (both free, apart from the entrance fee that each participant paid personally) – stayed online for two weeks and proved effective in reaching a large number of interested and in-target individuals. Candidates who had already participated in the museum cultural mediation experience were excluded from the research. Finally, a total of 35 interviews were undertaken. The group of participants was balanced in terms of background, gender, and age (ranging from 18 to 65 years old, although most of the interviewees were in the 20–35 age group), and – as preferred – heterogeneous in interests, artistic knowledge, and relational behaviours. A global and comprehensive understanding of museum cultural mediation was then made possible.

As a focal museum cultural mediation, Rome's National Gallery of Modern and Contemporary Art was adopted in this research project for four key reasons (see Chapter 1):

1 With its innovative display policies, it represents a challenging context for visitors where museum cultural mediation might be very helpful.
2 It focuses on modern and contemporary art, which is as attractive as it is demanding for non-expert individuals.
3 It recently designed museum cultural mediation experiences but still aims to move them forward in a continual strategy in order to adopt a visitor-orientation approach.
4 It participated in the project by sharing useful organizational information, such as mediator schedules.

After the recruitment phase, the participation of the individuals enrolled in the research project in museum cultural mediation experiences was scheduled and they took place throughout July 2021. To organize the schedule, the collaboration of both the museum and the mediator was invaluable: appointments with our participants were organized to include one or two of them for each experience to resemble as much as possible the real experience (consequently, the mediators knew about this research project and the participation of our subjects). On average, the museum cultural mediation lasted about two hours, in small groups of up to four people. Immediately after the experience, as previously agreed, participants were interviewed as informally as possible and in places where the participants felt comfortable (usually, nearby either in a cafe or in a quiet place). No interview lasted less than two hours, they were recorded, listened back to, and transcribed. This textual data was coded and systematically analysed to identify:

- Common patterns, metaphors, salient themes, and sub-themes (Zahradka and Sedlakova 2012).
- Attributes, benefits, and values according to the means-ends chain model. Finally, consensus maps were obtained along with the identification of several visitor clusters.

4.2.1 Findings: Decomposing Visitor Value

Overall, the research suggested some recurring themes in the way visitors consider the museum cultural mediation experience, which represents important aspects that need to be underlined.

- **The importance of free museum cultural mediation experience and advertising**

  Many interviewees emphasized the importance of a free museum cultural mediation experience and the relevance of communication. They see themselves as visitors who seek fun and entertainment in museum cultural mediation experiences; they are neither experts, nor necessarily art lovers and for this reason, they are not particularly willing to spend a large sum of money on the museum cultural mediation visit. For them, the fact the museum cultural mediation experience is free of charge is one of its most important attributes, providing the opportunity to do something new and fun at no extra cost. Without this incentive, they probably would not have considered this experience.

  "I saw that museum cultural mediation was included in the ticket price. This encouraged me a lot to take the mediation visit" (Franca, 39 years old).

  Furthermore, another important aspect for these inexperienced visitors is awareness of the museum cultural mediation experience.

Many of them knew what museum cultural mediation was but they were not aware that this could be experienced in that specific museum. Besides this, before starting the experience, they had trouble recognizing who the mediators were and who the visitors were. This fact demonstrates the need for proper communication policies both outside and inside the museum. As Lorenzo states:

> The experience was extremely positive; I will do it again (...) the only negative aspect occurred at the beginning of the visit. When I entered, I felt embarrassed, I was a little inexperienced and I didn't know how to acknowledge the mediator who would accompany me during the visit.
>
> (Lorenzo, 24 years old)

- **Museum cultural mediation increases interaction and creates emotions during the visit**

Different visitors placed particular emphasis on interaction and emotions during the visit. These two features are deeply linked to each other because the dialogue that takes place among visitors, who are strangers at the beginning of the visit, helps to break down the wall of shyness and to create bonds. It creates the basis for experiencing calm and for being transported elsewhere, carried away by emotions. Thanks to museum cultural mediation, people are not strangers any more as noted by Vanda:

> I was a little afraid of the mediation experience with a group of strangers; instead, then I changed my mind. The mediator was very good, he asked us questions to make us interact and understand what we perceived from the work.
>
> (Vanda, 60 years old)

- **Time management and route choice**

In general, the interviews enhanced the experience of museum cultural mediation with a series of positive aspects emerging. However, two aspects were particularly emphasized, namely time management and the choice of route made by the mediator. Time is a fundamental variable for the experience, and mediators should immediately inquire as to how much time visitors have available. This information is crucial in managing time accordingly, thus making the most of the experience. Overloading the visit with too many artworks to look at and overly complex information limits engagement in the museum cultural mediation. Sometimes, the experience was perceived as not very pleasant because it was too contrived, involved too much cognitive effort, or because the visitor did not have the opportunity and time to be able to linger on their favourite works. Luca and Carlotta explain this need well:

> During the visit, I was dragged around by the mediator, and I could not see any of the rooms I wanted to. I was not allowed to express my preferences regarding the route.
>
> (Luca, 30 years old)

> The saddest thing of all is that we visited some places in the gallery in a very hasty way as some of our group had very little time available. So, the fact that the visit takes some time needs to be clarified first, it's not meant to be a quick visit.
>
> (Carlotta, 34 years old)

- **Understanding the difference between museum mediator and museum guide**

  Before the visit experience and the interview, no theoretical explanation was ever given to the interviewed. However, despite such a low level of previous information, all the participants were able to correctly explain during the interviews what the role of the museum mediator was, and its differences compared to guides. Experiencing museum cultural mediation first-hand, they clarified, with interesting nuances, that museum mediators bring the general public closer to the arts, establishing a dialogue that provides the visitor with the necessary tools to personally understand the meanings of art.

4.2.2 Findings: Attributes, Benefits, and Values of Museum Cultural Mediation

The interviews provided rich data concerning the exploitation of visitor value from which the identification of attributes, benefits, and values follows.

Attributes of museum cultural mediation

- **Setting-up.** The setting-up of exhibitions represents the basis for exciting, reflective, and engaging experiences.
- **Companionship.** Participants highlight the role of the presence of others in the museum cultural mediation experience, i.e. one or more people with whom they are familiar and feel comfortable.
- **Temporary exhibitions.** This attribute expresses whether the works of art relate to a new exhibition or an exhibit with which the visitor is already familiar. It closely relates to an individual curiosity for discovery.

- **Mediator's age.** This attribute was noted because it can affect the visitor's decision to get involved and start a museum cultural mediation experience. Very often young mediators are associated – in the visitors' opinions – with little or no experience, along with lacking knowledge and professionalism. In this case, the visitor may be less likely to accept the experience.
- **Time management.** The experience is perceived as strongly dependent on the time management adopted by the mediators. This attribute influences both the quantity and the quality of the concepts learned. Museum cultural mediators must know how to manage time.
- **Free of charge.** Museum cultural mediation experiences included in the entrance fee may encourage visitors who are not fully tuned into museum cultural mediation to still find the offer beneficial.
- **Intimacy of the experience.** Museum cultural mediation experienced in very small groups (one or two people) is regarded as a prerequisite for greater visitor concentration and interaction with the mediator, making museum cultural mediation akin to a private experience.
- **Freedom of route.** Expert visitors especially know exactly where they want to go, and they often want to choose a route without any external interference. Thus, this attribute might be relevant.
- **Word of mouth.** This attribute is crucial because it drives awareness of museum cultural mediation. Moreover, it also relates to the trustworthiness of the person who motivates visitors to consider this experience.
- **Communication.** Like word of mouth, other communication policies can increase awareness and thus stimulate visitors to experience museum cultural mediation.
- **Quality of storytelling.** This attribute is regarded as essential to facilitate satisfying listening and experiences.
- **Quality of the exhibition route.** The choice of route made by the mediators is very important for participants. Many especially appreciate experiences hosted in rooms enriched by a clear and defined style. Perceived confusion, on the other hand, diminishes this.
- **Use of museum technologies.** Individuals favour the support of electronic and digital media. Since the visitor now acts as the main character in museum cultural mediation experiences, interactivity is essential to transform it into a personal event.

Benefits of museum cultural mediation

- **Approaching arts**. Participants stated that sometimes they need support in approaching works of art or museums. Even very interested visitors might perceive they lack the necessary skills and tools to understand. Thus, the fact that mediators build a bridge is greatly appreciated. The artworks, museums, and, in general, the arts, therefore, emerge as more approachable.
- **Involvement**. Museum cultural mediators are key drivers of visitor involvement.
- **Satisfied curiosity**. Visitors appreciate it when their curiosity is satisfied, and mediators can also stimulate them by boosting their interest in art, leading to an ever-increasing desire for knowledge.
- **Enjoyment**. This benefit is especially relevant for visitors who are not art enthusiasts as it makes the experience even more enjoyable and stimulating.
- **Emotions during the experience**. For many, this is the main benefit. This is what visitors say they expect from the visit.
- **Being listened to**. Visitors, especially those who have a broad cultural background (or at least think they have), aim to discuss art with the mediator. They want to talk about art, enjoy an exchange of opinion, and have the opportunity or space to express themselves.
- **Interaction**. During the visit, individuals want the opportunity to express themselves and converse with others. They aim to interact.
- **Feeling comfortable**. Visitors expect to be placed in a comfortable environment and to be welcomed by people that are suitable for their personalities and preferences.

Values of museum cultural mediation

- **Enrichment of cultural background**. Since many visitors do not feel they possess the required, in-depth knowledge on the subject, but remain interested in improving their knowledge through museum cultural mediation, this value is relevant in the findings.
- **Open-mindedness**. Acquiring knowledge over and beyond what they already possess is important for visitors. They enjoy the analysis of the works of art from different points of view. In this way, visitors acquire not only new knowledge but also a new aptitude for receiving opinions and experiencing the works of art through external stimuli.

- **Hedonism**. The museum cultural mediation experience creates important emotional drivers, which might even be more powerful than purely rational ones. Thus, hedonism is a key reference for some visitors.
- **Entertainment**. Finally, having an overall pleasurable experience drives some visitors, even though this may ignore the traditional elements of the visit, such as artistic content.

4.3 Findings: Four Customers Profiles of Museum Cultural Mediation

From an analysis of the means-ends chain, four groups of visitors emerge, resulting from the consensus maps: the curious visitor, the passionate visitor, the involved visitor, and the expert visitor.

1 The curious visitor

The first profile of visitors is mainly defined by curiosity in that they decide to experience the museum's cultural mediation because they are stimulated by communication from either the museum or other people. When visiting museums, their goal is to mainly have a pleasant experience, which does not necessarily depend on an interest in the artworks on display but rather on a need for entertainment (which can also be satisfied by watching a film at the cinema or a show at the theatre). They approach the museum's cultural mediation because they are invariably attracted by promotional touchpoints, which can be museum-owned (such as advertising), partner-owned (such as free services), visitor-owned (such as word of mouth or companionship), or even other-owned (such as the quality of storytelling). Regardless of the variety of touchpoints, these visitors seek interaction, are driven by curiosity and look for fun and entertainment in the museum's cultural mediation experience. Typically, these visitors experience museum cultural mediation for the first time, without any real or solid knowledge of the subject matter. Figure 4.1 represents the consensus map of this visitor segment.

2 The passionate visitor

The second visitor profile is the passionate visitor who is driven by curiosity in the subject and its innovativeness. This kind of visitor returns to the same museum several times to deepen their knowledge of the subject. Moreover, participating in the museum's cultural mediation represents a sort of personal hobby. The passionate visitor approaches the museum cultural mediation due

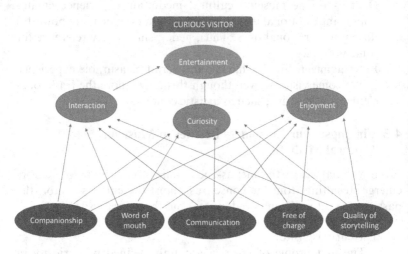

Figure 4.1 The consensus map of the curious visitor.
Source: Our elaboration.

to the appeal of the museum's set-up, as well as the mediator's knowledge and communication skills. Thus, the museum-owned touchpoints are especially relevant. In fact, these visitors are particularly stimulated by the use of technology and digital solutions that enrich the museum's cultural mediation, the quality of the storytelling, the intimacy of the visit, temporary exhibitions, and the management of the visiting time. Regardless of the heterogeneity of touchpoints, these visitors seek hedonism and enrichment of their cultural background through interaction with and understanding of the art experienced during the museum's cultural mediation. Typically, these visitors do not experience museum cultural mediation for the first time but possess sufficient knowledge of the topic. Figure 4.2 presents the consensus map of the passionate visitor.

3 The involved visitor

The third visitor profile is mainly defined by emotions and a desire to experience the museum's cultural mediation in search of hedonism. When visiting museums, involved visitors wish to have extremely moving experiences, to learn what kinds of feelings and emotions the arts arouse in them. Obviously, for this purpose, the mediator's role is essential: they must be able to provide visitors with appropriate stimuli. For this reason, the most important touchpoints are mainly the ones owned by the museum

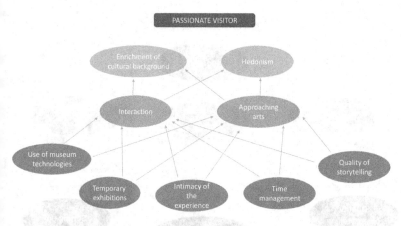

Figure 4.2 The consensus map of the passionate visitor.
Source: Our elaboration.

itself (quality of the storytelling, quality of the exhibition route, and the setting-up). Moreover, because of the wealth of emotions and sense of involvement experienced, this visitor profile is likely to talk about their experience afterwards. This tendency generates word of mouth, which belongs to the category of the partner-owned touchpoints. Furthermore, this visitor profile is likely to become a returning customer, looking for new emotions and experiences every time in a continual process towards engagement. Thus, museums dealing with this kind of audience should create differently themed museum cultural mediation experiences to satisfy the needs of this returning visitor. Figure 4.3 illustrates the consensus map of this profile.

4   The expert visitor

Finally, the expert visitor segment whose profile includes a very deep and broad cultural background. Moreover, expert visitors are constantly in search of new knowledge and want to discover different opinions and divergent perspectives on works of art. They are considered to be true experts on the subject and for them, any basic experience results in a feeling of failure; they are not satisfied with elementary museum cultural mediation experiences and expect to interact with qualified, professional, and prominent personalities in the surrounding environment. The main goal of expert visitors is to open their minds and this is why they are interested in museum cultural mediation. To that end,

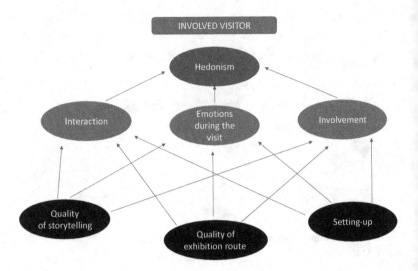

Figure 4.3 The consensus map of the involved visitor.
Source: Our elaboration.

they expect to feel at home, to be listened to, and to enjoy a profound interaction. Museum-owned touchpoints play a relevant
role in driving them, especially time management of the visit, the
intimacy of the visit, the mediator's age, and the freedom to decide which route to take. At the same time, they are also sensitive
to others-owned touchpoints, such as experts, critics, journalists,
and other museums that can stimulate their cognitive processes.
Typically, these visitors have experienced museum cultural mediation several times but without being regular participants. They
need a well-structured museum cultural mediation plan designed
especially for such a select group of experts. Figure 4.4 reports
their consensus map.

Figure 4.5 represents the key features of the 4 emerging visitor profiles.
Together, they identify 4 different targets related to the *a posteriori*
segmentation strategy for the museum cultural mediation experience.
As seen on the consensus maps, they differ from each other based
on their interest and knowledge regarding museum cultural mediation (and their field of application), the benefits that visitors expect to
reach, and the values that deeply differentiate each target. Whatever
application of museum cultural mediation is made, there will be an
audience stimulated to participate for different reasons.

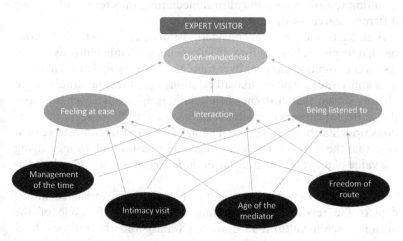

Figure 4.4 The consensus map of the expert visitor.
Source: Our elaboration.

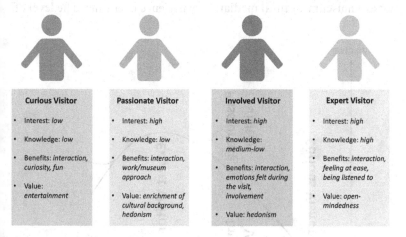

Figure 4.5 The four visitor profiles.
Source: Our elaboration.

4.4 The Evolutionary Museum Cultural Experience Model

Although the differences among the four visitor profiles are relevant, taken together they indicate a fundamental similarity: the four visitor profiles express disparate levels of the same concept, namely attention. The four kinds of visitors might be regarded as having distinct levels of attention towards museum cultural mediation, thus representing four different degrees of the same variable.

A global framework that considers visitor attention as the key variable that forms the basis of four different clusters is inherently dynamic. As visitor attention changes over time, the relationship between museums and visitors evolves, like all relationships. Previous studies have already shown that customer-firm relationships evolve over time and that different clusters of visitors emerge at different stages in the relationships (Blattberg, Getz, and Thomas 2001). In this context, we propose that the life cycle model can become a useful tool for measuring the value of a specific visitor: *the evolutionary museum cultural mediation experience model.*

The evolutionary museum cultural mediation experience model depicts the relationship over time between the life cycle of the visitor-museum cultural mediation (X-axis) and the visitor's level of attention (Y-axis). The latter results from interest, knowledge of museum cultural mediation, and number of previous museum cultural mediation experiences with the resulting curve describing the evolutionary museum cultural mediation experience over time. The level of

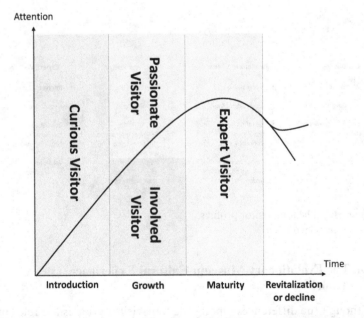

Figure 4.6 The evolutionary museum cultural mediation experience model.
Source: Our elaboration.

attention increases as time passes, representing the four visitor profiles as subsequent stages of the same curve (see Figure 4.6).

The different stages of the visitor's life cycle correspond to the four different clusters of visitors that require suitable managerial investments:

- **Introduction.** The curious visitor profile appears typically at the beginning of the relationship. In this introductory stage, visitors do not have much knowledge of artistic contents. To build the relationship, the museum cultural mediator must create interaction and harmony with the visitor. The main goal of museums is to entertain visitors during the experience by eliciting their curiosity and sense of fun. At this initial stage, it is also important to promote the museum's cultural mediation by way of touchpoints.
- **Growth.** At the growth stage, the relationship increases the level of attention. However, two profiles can emerge according to the relevance of the cognitive and emotional side to consumers. The passionate visitor profile represents visitors with a purely cultural-cognitive approach, whose visits increase over time if they can discover more art; at the same time, involved visitors appreciate the emotional side of the experience, returning if the museum stimulates them with different, experiential, and challenging offerings. Specifically, the 'passionate visitor' is very interested in the museum but is not an expert on the topics. For this reason, they seek interaction during the visit and a closer approach to the artwork or museum as an institution. Unlike the *previous visitor*, in this phase, the visitor wishes to enrich their cultural baggage and experience hedonism (strong emotional and cultural involvement) as final values. At the same time, the 'involved visitor' represents the group of visitors who most appreciate the emotional side of the visit, who typically turn into enthusiastic visitors. This visitor profile looks for involvement, interaction, emotions, and, ultimately, the value of hedonism. Positive feelings turn ordinary experiences into memorable ones.
- At the last stage (i.e. **maturity**), the visitors reach their highest level of attention, turning into 'expert visitors'. They represent a niche, featuring a strong interest in the works of art and the organization. They search for interaction, comfort, warmth, and profound dialogue that all facilitate the learning of new concepts. Thus, museums should support them in opening their minds and familiarizing themselves with new attitudes and approaches. This visitor profile is likely to appreciate mature mediators because of

the prejudice against the perceived limited skills of younger ones. The museum should address this issue and create solutions for readjusting the relationship between visitors and mediators.

- Each visitor presented could potentially belong to this phase because after their first museum cultural mediation experience, they may want to increase their knowledge through the various steps that museum cultural mediation training offers along the life cycle stages. The segmentation's main purpose is to ensure that, after the first visit, the visitor wants to have the experience again, through a differentiated and personalized museum cultural mediation offer. Thus, it would be appropriate to use:

- **Basic museum cultural mediation** for the 'introduction' phase which should consist of small group visits during which the mediator personally chooses the path and the works of art on which to linger. Before the visit, the mediator must inquire about the group's availability of time and must adapt the visit based on perceived interests.

- **Thematic paths** for the 'growth' phase, which consists of creating different theme-related itineraries: only a selected sample of works of art or rooms have to be included in the path, all consistent with the proposed theme. Thematic paths represent a pre-established type of museum cultural mediation. The creation of thematic itineraries encourages visitors to move towards museum cultural mediation, allowing them to gradually vary the type of visit.

- **Mediation days** for the 'maturity' phase whereby frequent museum cultural mediation days are recommended with leading professionals in the sector the museum is active in.

To date, a museum has been a place of cultural enrichment, where visitors ask to be involved and listened to in co-creative experiences. Understanding this audience demand allows the museum to develop the proper tools and then make them available to visitors. To reach this goal, museums – not only museum cultural mediation – should be visitor-oriented: this represents the real challenge.

Reference list

Arimond, G., and Elfessi, A. (2001). A clustering method for categorical data in tourism market segmentation research. *Journal of Travel Research, 39*(4), 391–397.

Bernard, H. (2017). *Research Methods in Anthropology: Qualitative and Quantitative Approaches.* Rowman & Littlefield: Lanham, MD.

Blattberg, R. C., Getz, G., and Thomas, J. S. (2001). *Customer Equity: Building and Managing Relationships as Valuable Assets.* Harvard Business Press: Boston, MA.

Botschen, G., Thelen, E. M., and Pieters, R. (1999). Using means-end structures for benefit segmentation: An application to service. *European Journal of Marketing, 33*(1/2), 38–58.

Boyce, C., and Neale, P. (2006). *Conducting In-Depth Interviews: A Guide for Designing and Conducting In-Depth Interviews for Evaluation Input.* Pathfinder international tool series, Monitoring and Evaluation – 2.

Budeva, D. G., and Mullen, M. R. (2014). International market segmentation: Economics, national culture, and time. *European Journal of Marketing, 48*(7/8), 1209–1238.

Burgess, M. M. (2007). Proposing modesty for informed consent. *Social Science & Medicine, 66*(11), 2284–2295.

Chen, Q., and Liu, Y. (2021). Research and analysis on the value of customer satisfaction in the environmental space of the museums. In *Proceedings of the 2nd International Conference on Language, Art and Cultural Exchange (ICLACE 2021)* (pp. 457–461). Atlantis Press: Amsterdam.

Colbert, F. (2017). A brief history of arts marketing thought in North America. *Journal of Arts Management, Law & Society, 47*(3), 167–177.

De Oliveira Castro, A. L., de Barros Vilas Boas, L. H., and Tonelli, D. F. (2018). Personal values, means end-chain, identity and consumption behavior in foods: A bibliometric review. *Revista Brasileira De Marketing, 17*(6), 771–787.

Donoghue, S. (2000). Projective techniques in consumer research. *Journal of Family Ecology and Consumer Sciences, 28*, 47–53.

Durgee, J. F. (1986). Self-esteem advertising. *Journal of Advertising, 15*(4), 21–42.

Green, P. E. (1977). A new approach to market segmentation. *Business Horizons, 20*(1), 61–73.

Haire, M. (1950). Projective techniques in marketing research. *Journal of Marketing, 14*(5), 649–656.

Holbrook, M. B, and Morris, B. (1999). *Consumer Value: A Framework for Analysis and Research.* Psychology Press: Hove, East Sussex.

Jooyeon, H., and SooCheong, J. (2013). Attributes, consequences, and consumer values: A means-end chain approach across restaurant segments. *International Journal of Contemporary Hospitality Management, 25*(3), 383–409.

Levitt, T. (1965). Exploit the product life cycle. *Harvard Business Review, 43*, 81–94.

McKenzie-Mohr, D., and Wesley Schultz, P. (2014). Choosing effective behaviour change tools. *Social Marketing Quarterly, 20*(1), 35–46.

Modesto Veludo-de-Oliveira, T., et al. (2006). Laddering in the practice of marketing research: Barriers and solutions. *Qualitative Market Research: An International Journal, 9*(3), 297–306.

Morar, D. (2013). *An Overview of the Consumer Value Literature – Perceived Value, Desired Value.* In *International Conference "Marketing – from information to decision" at Cluj-Napoca, 6.* Accessed on August 21, 2022. Available at: https://www.researchgate.net/publication/271585009_An_overview_of_the_consumer_value_literature_-_perceived_value_desired_value

Nunkoo, R., and Ramkissoon, H. (2009). Applying the means-end chain theory and the laddering technique to the study of host attitudes to tourism. *Journal Sustainable Tourism, 17*(3), 337–355.

Perkins, W. S., and Reynolds, T. J. (1988). The explanatory power of values in preference judgements: Validation of the means-end perspective. *Advanced in Consumer Research, 15*(1), 122–126.

Reynolds, T. J., and Olson, J. C. (2001). *Understanding Consumer Decision Making: The Means End Approach to Marketing and Advertising Strategy.* Lawrence Erlbaum Associates Publishers: Mahwah, NJ.

Ritchie, J., et al. (2013). *Qualitative Research Practice: A Guide for Social Science Students and Researchers.* SAGE Publications: Thousand Oaks, CA.

Tasci, A. (2016). A critical review of consumer value and its complex relationships in the consumer-based brand equity network. *Journal of Destination Marketing & Management, 5*(3), 171–191.

Weinstein, A. (2004). *Handbook of Market Segmentation: Strategic Targeting for Business and Technology Firms.* Taylor & Francis – Routledge: New York.

Xiao, L., and Guo, Z. (2018). Benefit-based O2O commerce segmentation: A means-end chain approach. *Electronic Commerce Research, 19*(2), 409–49.

Zahradka, P., and Sedlakova, R. (2012). *New Perspectives on Consumer Culture Theory and Research.* Cambridge Scholars Publishing: Newcastle Upon Tyne.

5 The Customized Model of Museum Cultural Mediation

Walter Altamirano Aguilar
and Valeria Bellusci

5.1 Defining a New Type of Museum Visit

Recently, the ability of traditional, museum-guided tours to reach new segments of the public has been widely questioned (Black 2005; Falk and Dierking 2010). For a considerable amount of time, the main intermediary role between cultural heritage and visitors – and in a broader sense between the museum and the public – was the guided tour. Traditionally, guided tours aim to provide the visitor with historical notions to deliver the value of cultural heritage, which is rich in seemingly unambiguous and unquestionable meanings. From this perspective, the visitor's point of view appears to be irrelevant, with an indistinct and homogenous audience. This type of visit would no longer appear to meet visitors' needs as recent socio-cultural changes show (Varnum and Grossmann 2017). Museums are called upon to advance their role and, above all, to rethink their relationship with visitors. To engage their audience, museums must respond to the specific needs of individual visitors (Silverman 1995; Weil 1997) and consider visitor orientation as the central approach to their activity (Hooper-Greenhill 1994; Weil 1997). Weil (1997) predicted that the relationship between museums and audiences would reach a state where "it will be the public, not the museum, that occupies the superior position. The museum's role will have been transformed from one of mastery to one of service" (p. 257). Only by considering visitors' points of view, can museums obtain the interest of a wider variety of visitors and offer them valuable, enjoyable, and at the same time educational experiences (Reussner 2003). Nowadays, a new kind of experience based on more emotional and experiential engagement has emerged (Kotler 2008). Indeed, Ryan et al. (2010) highlight that

> When users take an active role in the shape of art performance and service delivery, it becomes generally difficult to define

DOI: 10.4324/9781003352754-5

controlled sequential and scripted experiences. This means that the experience cannot be pre-defined, including where the art is located, when it starts or when it will end.

(p. 222)

This new kind of museum orientation fits in well with the broad and competitive leisure market, as well as responding to new environmental challenges (Hanquinet 2013). Visitors have changed their expectations related to the museum experience (Bello and Matchette 2018); they are eager to know but at the same time they wish to be questioned, listened to, and facilitated to find their way around independently (Carù and Cova 2005).

5.2 Benefits and Values of Visitors in Museum Cultural Mediation

The four identified profiles of visitors rely on the benefits and values sought. Mediators should plan museum visits according to the characteristics of each visitors' profile. The aim is customizing the visitor experience through the skills they received training for (see Chapter 3). Museum cultural mediation facilitates the achievement of benefits and values for the visitors and plays a truly innovative role within public services by bringing the needs of the public to the centre of the visitor experience (Morsch and Holland 2013). The qualitative research presented in Chapter 4, in line with the literature, highlights two-character traits that emerge as crucial and represent primary differences from the traditional guided tour.

The first significant characteristic of museum cultural mediation is the degree of participation established with the visitors, a sought-after benefit common to all four profiles deriving from the analysis. Due to the extreme importance of visitors' desires to be listened to, to interact, and to be involved, museum cultural mediation is relatively effective in satisfying them by stimulating interactive participation. The latter has important consequences such as the audience's active role and co-creative experiences, as well as a continual revision of the content of the museum cultural mediation itself.

The second important feature of museum cultural mediation is the opportunity to engage various profiles of visitors thanks to their ability to focus on different benefits, arising from the audience's desired values and the possibility of achieving them. Indeed, museum cultural mediation can communicate multiple value propositions driven by visitor characteristics. As was clear from visitor interviews, each profile features different values, attributable to the categories of *'entertainment'*, *'hedonism'*, *'cultural enrichment'*, and *'open-mindedness'* (see Chapter 4). Through cultural mediation, museums can offer customized visitor routes for the four identified profiles. To that end, museums must embrace a visitor-centred approach, called upon to recognize their significant values. Thanks to their skills, cultural mediators can help visitors to find these benefits in cultural experiences. Because of a greater openness to visitor relationships, these two major characteristics (namely, degree of participation and value propositions) can enable museum cultural mediation to achieve a broader range of objectives and results than any other educational or entertainment service.

5.3 Customized Museum Cultural Mediation

A single solution to attract and satisfy all profiles of visitor, of course, does not exist. Indeed, museums should focus on the different degrees of attention of the four profiles of visitors to engage them, as already discussed in Chapter 4 that mentions the 'visitor cycle'. Since the level of attention is determined by visitors' degree of interest and prior knowledge, along with benefits and values sought, the museum must leverage these variables according to the different types of visitors. In the previous section, the ability of cultural mediators to establish a relationship through the degree of participation and the value proposition was emphasized. However, museum cultural mediation establishes engagement with visitors by enhancing all the variables that make up the degree of attention. Cultural mediators, through their skills, can focus primarily on the variables just described and thus conduct a different type of museum cultural mediation for visitors each and every time. The four visitor profiles, identified through a qualitative research project, and the mediators' capabilities developed in the educational programmes, analysed by way of benchmarking analysis, represent the input for a customized model of museum cultural mediation. This adopts a marketing approach whereby the visitors and their needs define the kind of museum cultural mediation used. As each of the four visitor profiles seeks different benefits and has different values, customization of the museum cultural mediation is thereby made possible. Four different kinds of cultural mediators emerge: the *'Educator Mediator'*, the *'Designer Mediator'*, the *'Guide Mediator'*, and the *'Manager Mediator'*. These four profiles differ in their degree of expertise in the four areas of competency and the target: the *'Educator'*, the *'Designer'*, and the *'Guide'* approach visitors directly while the *'Manager'* addresses museum cultural mediators directly. They are defined as follows:

1 Educator Mediator

The first kind of museum cultural mediator is called the *'Educator Mediator'* for whom *pedagogic* and communicative skills are crucial. They provide visitors with the essential information to understand contents without excessive details. To that end, they can establish trustworthy relationships with the public, engaging them, exchanging ideas, and creating interaction. Thus, they lead experiences designed to attract the visitor's attention through planned routes where several visitor characteristics can act as segmentation criteria. The *'Educator'* focuses on the visitor's degree of interest and stimulates reflection by encouraging a personal elaboration of cultural heritage in a comfortable environment that is rich in *informality* and *spontaneity.*

The visitor's perception should be of a shared experience, where playful and interactive elements are invaluable. To further enhance the tour, people must participate directly in designing the visiting experience, for example, by choosing a thematic itinerary.

Matching the Educator Mediator with Museum Visitors' Profiles

The audience that suits the *'Educator Mediator'* is fun-seeking and wishes to experience a visit emotionally. Their interest and prior knowledge levels might be low or high-low, therefore, the *'Educator Mediator'* matches the *'Involved Visitor'* and the *'Curious Visitor'*. During a tour with the *'Involved Visitor'*, they can focus on some museum pieces and stimulate reflection by leveraging an emotional response. This calls for attention to be paid to the visitors' reactions and requires them to be engaged in a dialogue on the aspects that most affect the viewer. For instance, given the greater inclination of the *'Involved'* towards cultural heritage, the *'Educator'* should focus on historical and anthropological notions.

Similarly, informal dialogue and emotional interaction are key aspects to triggering the interest of *'Curious Visitors'*. For example, after an initial general overview of the museum collection, the *'Educator'* will discover which museum collection pieces generate interest the most and discuss them with the *'Curious'* audience. Once attention has been gained, the *'Educator'* should try to elicit curiosity in pieces which were initially judged not to the taste of the *'Curious'*. Furthermore, since this profile of visitor tends not to come to the museum alone, the *'Educator'* can also foster interaction within the group itself. The *'Educator'* is skilled at keeping the conversation away from technical or formal details which might turn the *'Curious'* and the *'Involved'* off the idea of approaching the museum's cultural exhibition.

2 Designer Mediator

The second type of cultural mediator is called *'Designer Mediator'*, who is needed where museography skills are at the core. They establish a relationship of trust with the public by engaging them throughout the museum environment.

The role of the *'Designer'* is to immerse the visitors in an experience that enhances the tangible aspects of the museum visit, which means not only with the museum collection but also within the unique surrounding environment. Communication skills and an in-depth knowledge of the museum's vision enable the *'Designer'* to contextualize cultural heritage and stimulate the visitor's imagination. Their role, therefore, becomes increasingly central when the architecture or the context of the museum itself is crucial to an all-round understanding of the visit. Starchitects' buildings or museums which are part of wider archaeological sites are just an example of how indispensable it is to enhance the complete enjoyment of the cultural heritage in question. In addition to that, the *'Designer'* is characterized by an excellent knowledge of multimedia languages and tools that can stimulate the visitor's active participation in the audience engaged.

To further improve the experience, the visitor will deepen their understanding of cultural heritage through the quality of storytelling.

Matching the Designer Mediator with museum visitors' profiles

The *'Designer'* is suitable for those visitors who seek an emotional angle to enrich their knowledge of cultural heritage and are willing to explore new ways of enjoying it. Visitor interest and prior knowledge levels are high-low or high-medium, therefore, the *'Designer Mediator'* matches the *'Passionate Visitor'* and *'Involved Visitor'*. The *'Designer'* succeeds in stimulating visitors by making the *'Passionate'* and the *'Involved'* visitor identify with the museum's vision also through the help of technological tools to support the exhibition. The *'Passionate'*, invariably attracted to storytelling, may be captivated by the description of the surroundings and the relationships between the museum collection pieces during the visit. It is important for the *'Passionate'* to be helped to mentally reconstruct the historical context to enhance their degree of interest and appreciation. Moreover, multimedia support is useful for enriching the original context of the cultural heritage and portraying it in a contemporary museum setting. The '*Involved*' has less interest in deepening knowledge but instead seeks engagement through the quality of storytelling and participation. Indeed, they desire an experience characterized by values and highly positive emotions: storytelling subjects can be inspired by contemporary lifestyle and current trends. The '*Designer*' can guide the '*Involved*' through museum multimedia tools into a more evocative visit experience.

3   Guide Mediator

The third type of museum cultural mediator is called '*Guide Mediator*' who performs a function where notional skills are at the core. They will establish a relationship of trust with the audience by increasing the visitors' knowledge, as well as holding conversations and debating cultural heritage.

Their role seems to be very much in line with that of a traditional guide in that both start from a deep, technical, and theoretical knowledge of what they present to the public and base their visit mainly around a very one-sided flow of information. However, the difference from the latter is substantially found in the approach taken and in the relationship established with the visitor. In museum cultural mediation, the hierarchical gap that usually exists between museum guide and visitor is bridged, thanks to the communicative and didactic expertise acquired from training courses and then developed with experience. The communicative register relinquishes a formal tone and the unnecessary use of technicalities that can characterize traditional guided tours and reduces the barriers with visitors by making them feel at ease and encouraging them to express queries and questions. The profound knowledge of cultural heritage, combined with better communication skills, provides visitors with all the key ingredients to understand the work, keeping their attention and curiosity levels high. The skill of the '*Guide*' lies in adapting register, topics, and explanation to the audience, whilst at the same time openly engaging with them to respond to the queries, questions and needs of the visitors.

The visitors will perceive a highly educational, intimate experience that frees them to choose the most suitable visit path.

Matching the Guide Mediator with museum visitors' profiles

The typical drivers of visitors for the '*Guide*' are the desire to enrich their knowledge about cultural heritage and to talk with fellow experts about cultural heritage as their level of interest and prior knowledge is either high-medium or high. Indeed, suitable visitors for the *'Guide'* show themselves to be primarily attentive to the quality and quantity of the notions communicated relating to cultural heritage. Therefore, the *'Guide Mediator'* matches the *'Expert Visitor'* and the *'Passionate Visitor'* for their ability to respond to curiosity and to the desire to go into detail: their expertise in cultural heritage is best suited to capture the attention of visitors with a generally high level of interest in art but who may however differ in terms of their prior knowledge of the museum collection. The *'Guide'* leaves the *'Expert Visitor'* free to choose which route to take and which pieces to focus on. Moreover, the *'Expert'* is eager to share their knowledge and be listened to. During the whole visit, the 'Guide' shall shape the visit in line with the visitors' interventions, striking a balance between listening and speaking. Being ready to answer more specific questions is crucial in order not to risk being assessed as inadequate by the *'Expert'*. Instead, the *'Passionate Visitor'* who is defined by a basic knowledge of the museum collection, pays more attention to the quality of storytelling, and has a strong desire to boost their cultural background through the visit. The *'Guide'* must fine-tune ideas to the knowledge level of their interlocutor to stimulate dialogue and discussion. Therefore, developing interaction allows both the *'Expert'* and the *'Passionate'* to get closer to the museum collection.

4 Manager Mediator

The fourth type of cultural mediator is called *'Manager Mediator'* who performs a function where legal and economic skills are fundamental. The museum cultural mediators described above meet the visitors' sought-after benefits and especially values, which are the determining factor in their choice of visit. The need for museums to identify the values of current and potential visitors raises questions related to which figure is best suited to perform this task. This choice can lead to a hierarchy of the importance of value propositions due to multiple factors (i.e. budgeting, staffing, museum strategy). A figure capable of mediating between the different interests in play and of helping the Head of the Mediation Service develop a proper communication strategy is the *'Manager'* mediator, whose fundamental skills are legal and economic. Their duties include designing cultural mediation activities, defining the selection criteria for cultural mediators, and developing audience-targeted activities that consider the use of technologies in the museum, the attributes of temporary and permanent exhibitions, the physical spaces available, quality, and type of storytelling adopted, and museum positioning.

More generally, the '*Manager*' is responsible for coordinating the different museum cultural mediators and enhancing the work of other mediators. They address and evaluate the performance of museum cultural mediation services, preparing reports and feedback processes, both internally and externally. They understand

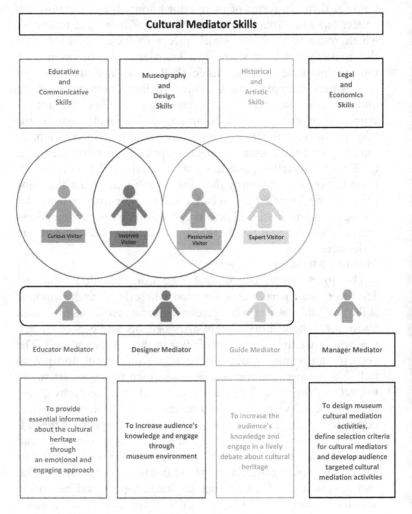

Figure 5.1 Cultural mediator skills and functions.
Source: Our elaboration.

the needs of new audiences and solve the museum's issues in consolidating the relationship with current audiences and attracting new visitors.

Therefore, the *'Manager'* is not associated with any specific audience but rather with the cultural mediators themselves: the *'Educator'*, the *'Designer'*, and the *'Guide'* (Figure 5.1).

5.4 Museum Cultural Mediation as a Tool for Audience Engagement

Despite the important differences among the four kinds of cultural mediators, they all share a common feature: the core role of the visitor's participation in the cultural experience. For each profile of audience, the need to be heard, involved, and questioned emerges as central to museum cultural mediation, regardless of any other specific detail. The demand for a dynamic and interactive visiting experience where the visitor is called upon to play an active role defines a new paradigm of museum experience far removed from the static nature of traditional guided tours. The ability of the museum to respond to this demand becomes central to this new museum reality, exemplified by a visitor-centred approach. Museums are called upon to increase and enhance their audience engagement tools to respond to this need for audience participation. Engagement is a psychological condition resulting from highly interactive, dynamic, co-creative, and relational customer experiences (Brodie et al. 2011), and previous analyses have highlighted the dynamic, interactive, and relational aspects characterizing museum cultural mediation. This is the key difference between museum cultural mediation and the traditional guided tour. Only an engaged audience is willing to share its knowledge and participate in activities proactively, as museum cultural mediation requires. Audience engagement driven by co-creative experiences leads to visitor satisfaction and loyalty (Banyte and Dovaliene 2014). Also, Flint et al. (2010) find that the ability to anticipate customers' desires (i.e., customer value anticipation) *"is a strong driver of satisfaction and loyalty, with satisfaction acting as a mediator for loyalty"* (p. 219). Interaction, co-creation, and value propositions are the fundamentals of the museum cultural mediator-visitor relationship. To that end, museum cultural mediation becomes a tool that can effectively achieve audience engagement. Indeed, it must be customized according to specific visitor value by recognizing visitor profiles as an important ingredient in museum cultural mediation.

5.5 The Three-Stage Model of the Visitor Experience

According to the three-stage model of the visitor experience developed by Sheng and Chen (2011), museum cultural mediation should leverage several elements to identify visitor profiles, as represented in Figure 5.2, and presented here according to the visit stage:

5.5.1 Pre-Visit Stage

At this stage, four visitor variables are key:

*   Level of interest
*   Visitors' prior knowledge
*   Desired benefits
*   Values

The existence and combination of these variables for each visitor profile establish a different kind of development in museum cultural mediation. Specifically, Taheri (2011) analysed and tested the effect of prior knowledge, learning-oriented motivation, enjoyment-oriented motivation, and cultural capital on the level of engagement. These aspects will define the structure of the museum cultural mediation. Before the visit begins, cultural mediators ask visitors some questions in order to understand the visitors' traits. Questions might regard:

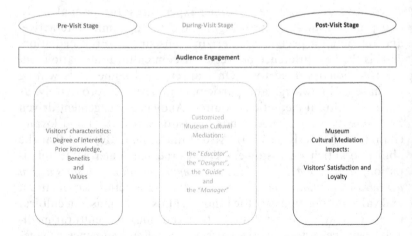

Figure 5.2 Museum cultural mediation through a three-stage model of the visitor experience.

Source: Our elaboration.

- What the visitor is looking for from the visit experience.
- What the degrees of prior knowledge and interest are.
- The amount of time available to the visitor.

Based on the answers, the museum cultural mediator must associate the visitor with one of the visitor profiles and develop cultural mediation accordingly. Other questions that can serve a purpose to this end concern:

- Whether it is the visitor's first time to the museum.
- Whether they came intending to see the permanent collection or the temporary exhibition.
- Whether they agree to visit the museum rooms in a general way and to focus only on the main pieces in the collection.

For example, a *'Curious Visitor'*, characterized by low levels of interest and low-prior knowledge, will be focused on the more general aspects of the experience and more inclined to seek entertainment during the visit. In this case, the cultural mediator should try to minimize theoretical notions and leverage interaction, storytelling, encouragement of new interpretations and an active involvement of the visitor through association games.

5.5.2 During-Visit Stage

This is a fundamental phase of the visitor experience because it is at this stage that the visitor-cultural mediator relationship is established for the benefit of audience engagement. Cultural mediators must recognize the visitors' characteristics (i.e. level of interest, prior knowledge, desired benefits, and sought values) and leverage them for an engaging visitor experience. The cultural mediator at this stage will pose more specific, more targeted questions (depending on how the visitor reacts during the visit) that should allow them to confirm the visitor categorization made at the previous stage. For example, they might ask questions regarding the themes of permanent or temporary exhibitions or their interpretation of the museum collection. They will also suggest viewing museum rooms based on the visitor interests expressed during the visit so far. Indeed, this is a fundamental phase of the visitor experience where the mediator's ability to understand non-verbal signals through listening, observation and empathy facilitate their relationship with visitors. This aspect was recognized by a couple of senior mediators interviewed at the National Gallery of Modern and Contemporary Art in Rome. Mariangela commented:

> It is crucial for a mediator to be empathetic. The mediator should understand the visitor in front of him and approach each person differently. They must be aware of the audience's signals and understand if the visitor is losing interest or is tired. They must pay attention to the audience and their needs and guide them in their visit and keep their attention high.
>
> (Mariangela, senior cultural mediator)

Caterina added:

> I try to leave a lot of room for people as a matter of empathy. I don't impose my views and I understand how they are behaving with me. I don't try to harass them with questions or to give them just a guided tour. I leave them in their comfort zone and try to fit in. I venture a few different notions, not just aesthetic or thematic.
>
> (Caterina, senior cultural mediator)

5.5.3 Post-Visit Stage

This stage establishes a starting point for building a relationship outside the museum with the audience. It starts with the end of the visit when it is fundamental for cultural mediators to ask for feedback on the museum but especially on the mediation experience. Questions might regard: (1) whether they felt comfortable during the visit; (2) what they appreciated the most; and (3) whether they would be willing to come back to repeat the experience. Feedback tools (i.e. questionnaires, surveys, interviews) can guarantee a definition of the strengths and weaknesses of museum cultural mediation to help rethink the structure, finetuning the visitor experience according to changes in audience demands. As demonstrated by visitor interviews, the impact on the public of museum cultural mediation turns out to be positive. Indeed, a long-lasting impact includes the possibility of maintaining direct contact between visitors and the museum's cultural mediators. This is also recognized by mediators themselves, working at the National Gallery of Modern and Contemporary Art, who said:

> There was a couple, she was studying architecture and had an exam in Contemporary Art History, which is why she came [...] she spoke and I added more information. [...] We even exchanged

numbers and she wrote to me to continue the exchange of ideas and information.

(Stephanie, senior cultural mediator)

This point is also raised by Caterina:

Some of the guys were very happy [...] we were like three friends taking a tour of the museum. Then they followed me on Instagram and now we keep in touch from time to time.

(Caterina, senior cultural mediator)

5.6 Enhancing the Cultural Heritage through Audience Development Drivers

More generally, museum cultural mediation promotes a new kind of visit responsive to visitors' demands. Therefore, museum cultural mediators must foresee a set of variables to satisfy the visitor's search for a personal experience. Specifically, several drivers emerge from the literature review as particularly relevant for the contribution of museum cultural mediation to audience engagement.

Museum-Based Drivers:

- **Visitor Entertainment** is accomplished through a new way of enjoying cultural heritage based on an interactive and participatory experience, combined with educational and playful moments.
- **Co-creation** highlights a new interpretation of the museum visiting experience. The visitor is called upon to be an integral part of shaping the museum's cultural mediation, sharing reflections, interpretations and states of mind. Cultural mediators play a fundamental role in making the visitor feel at ease, allowing them to express themselves freely and play an active part in designing the visit experience.

Context-Based Drivers:

- **Physical Context** is where the museum cultural mediation takes place. In the dialogue between cultural heritage and the architectural space, mediators assume one of their major functions: they become a medium between the museum, cultural heritage and the general public. Thus, the mediator must succeed in highlighting curatorial choices and allowing for the possibility to read the cultural heritage within the museum space.

* **Social Context** is how the museum's cultural mediation comes to life and is expressed. The exchange of ideas and reflections and interaction among visitors are stimuli for the promotion of a dynamic experience. Cultural mediators must incentivize dialogue and interaction not only between themselves and the individual visitor but also among the visitors.

Visitor Based Drivers:

* **Visitors' characteristics** are aspects that define the relationship with the cultural mediators and the value proposition of the visit. Indeed, visitors' characteristics define the emotions and level of involvement for each type of mediation.
* **Visitor's emotions** and **involvement** make the visit more experiential. Emphasizing the emotional aspects of the visitors allows them to immerse themselves in an experience that places their subjectivity at the centre.

In the *'Pre-visit stage'* the *'Visitor-based'* drivers are fundamental and will be understood in advance to structure the type of museum cultural mediation best suited to the visitor. Then, the core of the museum cultural mediators, emerging in the *'During-visit stage'*, is to enable the public to find their expected benefits according to their values. At this stage, the mediator leverages the *'Museum-based'* and *'Context-based'* drivers to lead the visit experience. Finally, the *'Post-visit stage'* includes all the perceptions, sensations, and thoughts that have arisen during the experience and must be documented in order to continually improve the service. Therefore, the museum cultural mediators – aimed at achieving customer's satisfaction and loyalty – should ask for, evaluate visitors' feedbacks and accordingly finetune the museum cultural mediation to the visitors' demands.

5.7   Designing a Customized Cultural Mediation Model

Proposing museum cultural mediation as a new engagement tool attempts to answer the fresh challenges posed by the entertainment market and the cultural sector. A visitor-oriented approach is necessary to respond to new audience demands and to establish a stable and long-lasting relationship with them. To clarify the previous analysis, the pivotal decision-making moments in defining a museum cultural mediation experience are retraced: from knowing the audience to establishing feedback processes. Designing a museum cultural mediation experience means addressing the aspects that concern the phase preceding, during, and following the visit. Figure 5.3 shows a decision tree that highlights the aspects the museum must evaluate to define a mediation system that is aligned with its visitor orientation approach. The crucial decision points for the museum are highlighted through the following six steps.

1 Knowing the audience

Museum cultural mediation aims to build a museum visit experience that is customized to visitors' needs and values. Therefore, it is necessary to start from the audience's knowledge in order to understand visitors' demands, allowing for the customization of the experience. Understanding the audience and its value chain is possible through qualitative analysis (i.e. in-depth interviews) addressed at samples of museum visitors. In the event the museum already has information regarding its audience and its use of services, the *a priori model* would appear to be the most immediate and least costly choice. On the other hand, where the goal is to introduce a new service to the public, as was the case in the current research for cultural mediation, an *a posteriori segmentation model* is inevitable (Arimond and Elfessi 2001, Budeva and Mullen 2014). The advantages of *a posteriori* segmentation are numerous, including greater precision and greater effectiveness in formulating marketing strategy and the offering formula. Bernard (2017) emphasized that the starting point is the identification of attributes from the visitor's point of view. The attributes are selected, elicited, classified, and scaled by way of appropriate procedures.

Since the goal is to investigate individual attitudes, behaviours, and preferences in preparing questions, two kinds of techniques can be especially useful: the *'projective'* (Donoghue 2000) and the *'laddering technique'* (Modesto et al. 2006). These techniques are not used to measure but to uncover feelings, beliefs, attitudes, and motivations that many consumers might find difficult to articulate.

2 Defining visitor profiles

Qualitative analysis allows for the segmentation of the audience into different visitor profiles. Each category should identify precise benefits, values, levels of interest, as well as prior knowledge. Visitor value analysis is crucial for a comprehensive understanding of visitors' subjective preferences (Holbrook and Morris 1999),

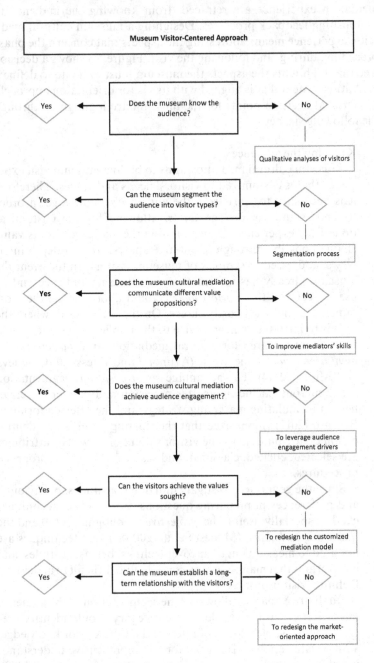

Figure 5.3 Decision-making flowchart.
Source: Our elaboration.

with relevant positive effects for the development of successful long-term museum cultural mediation experiences. The profiles of visitors later become the targets to customize the experience. Whatever typology is adopted, scholars of consumer behaviour and marketing agree that values need to be decomposed to measure visitor value, which is composed of expected or perceived benefits as well as sacrifices to be made by the visitor (which might be either tangible or intangible) (Tasci 2016). Museum cultural mediation is no exception: visitor value analysis of museum cultural mediation is expected to identify the specific values that drive preferences, satisfaction, engagement and any other attitudinal or behavioural visitor response. Thus, value analysis of visitors towards museum cultural mediation offers precious insights on how to segment the market and design successful and engaging visitor experiences.

3 Communicating different value propositions

Only by considering the visitors' point of view, can museums gain the interest of a variety of visitors and offer them valuable, enjoyable and, at the same time, educational experiences (Reussner 2003). Indeed, Flint et al. (2010) find that the ability to anticipate customers' desires (i.e. customer value anticipation) *"is a strong driver of satisfaction and loyalty, with satisfaction acting as a mediator for loyalty"* (p. 219). When it comes to the example of museum cultural mediation, it must be able to communicate value propositions based on the specific profile of visitors. They seek different benefits and values which are achievable through the mediator's ability to conduct a customized museum cultural mediation and to communicate the value proposition best suited to the visitor. Therefore, it is necessary for cultural mediators to be properly trained in the following areas of expertise:

• Historical and artistic
• Education and communication
• Mseography and design
• Legal and economic

These, according to the value sought by the visitor profiles, define the function of the mediators: 'Guide', 'Educator', 'Designer', and 'Manager Mediator'.

4 Achieving audience engagement

Customers prefer cultural offerings that include active participation, interaction and, if possible, co-creation (Styvén 2010).

Co-creation is a key driver of audience engagement, both in the value creation and value delivery processes (Addis 2020). As emphasized earlier, museum cultural mediation develops in a cultural mediator-visitor relationship, which leverages aspects such as participation, interaction, and co-creation. To identify museum cultural mediation as a visitor engagement tool implies objectives such as visitor satisfaction and loyalty (Banyte and Dovaliene 2014). In the case of the customized museum cultural mediation model, this means proposing a specific value proposition for each type of visitor and exact benefits during the visit stage. To communicate the value propositions and provide visitor benefits, the cultural mediator must leverage many of the drivers of audience engagement: **Museum-based**, **Context-based**, and **Visitor-based**. Finally, a combination of their abilities and the enhancement of audience engagement drivers enable museum cultural mediation to establish an engaging relationship with the audience.

5   Achieving the visitor values sought

The conclusion of the visit does not end the process of museum cultural mediation. As the three-stage model of the visitor experience developed by Sheng and Chen (2011) shows, at the next stage, a visitor's memories and feelings related to the experience become crucial in evaluating the visit itself. Through the feedback tools offered by the museum, it is possible to understand how and whether the museum achieved visitor satisfaction. This means understanding whether the visitors obtained the values and benefits sought. Any failure by the audience to obtain these values may highlight errors in the design of the museum cultural mediation model. These can occur in audience segmentation and the cultural mediators' approaches to conducting the visit. Therefore, feedback tools (such as questionnaires, surveys, interviews, or other evaluation tools) are needed in order to understand visitors' perceptions of museum cultural mediation. The skills of the mediator manager, in line with the museum's perspective, must entail a rethink of the museum's cultural mediation structure (i.e. defining mediator selection criteria, redefining internal mediator training, creating new activities) by responding to rapid changes in audience demands.

6   Establishing a long-term relationship with the visitor

A continual *improvement in the service based on visitor demands creates the conditions for developing a stable and long-lasting relationship between the general public and the museum. By enhancing visitor* characteristics and aspects of the visit identified as drivers of engagement, museum cultural mediation shows itself to be an effective visitor engagement tool aimed at visitor satisfaction and loyalty. Through the achievement of the values pursued by the visitor and the proposition of a new visiting experience, the museum can redefine its relationship with the public. By influencing the public's visiting experience, museum cultural mediation affects the visitor's perception of the museum itself, from a place of preservation of cultural heritage to a space capable of providing a new and engaging experience. Museum cultural mediation aims:

- To discover the profile of visitors.
- To segment several types of audience.
- To propose value propositions based on visitor characteristics.
- To engage audiences through drivers that have emerged from the literature.
- To establish a long-term relationship with visitors.

These represent the most important and critical issues for a museum adopting a visitor-oriented approach. Ultimately, museum cultural mediation represents a tool with the ability to enhance and manage every step necessary in order to achieve a market-oriented approach for museums.

Reference list

Addis, M. (2020). *Engaging Brands*. Taylor & Francis – Routledge: London.

Arimond, G., and Elfessi, A. (2001). A clustering method for categorical data in tourism market segmentation research. *Journal of Travel Research, 39*(4), 391–397.

Banyte, J., and Dovaliene, A. (2014). Relations between customer engagement into value creation and customer loyalty. *Procedia – Social and Behavioral Sciences, 156*, 484–489.

Bello, J., and Matchette, S. (2018). *Shifting Perspectives: The Millennial Influence on Museum Engagement*. In *Theory and Practice, 1*. Accessed on July 29, 2022. Available at: https://articles.themuseumscholar.org/2018/06/11/tp_vol1bellomatchette.

Bernard, H. R. (2017). *Research Methods in Anthropology: Qualitative and Quantitative Approaches*. Rowman & Littlefield: Washington DC.

Black, G. (2005). *The Engaging Museum: Developing Museums for Visitor Involvement*. Taylor & Francis – Routledge: London.

Brodie, R. J., et al. (2011). Customer engagement: Conceptual domain, fundamental propositions, and implications for research. *Journal of Service Research, 14*(3), 252–271.

Budeva, G.D., and Mullen, R.M. (2014). International market segmentation economics national culture and time. *European Journal of Marketing, 48*(7/8), 1209–238.

Carù, A., and Cova, B. (2005). The impact of service elements on the artistic experience: The case of classical music concerts. *International Journal of Arts Management, 7*(2), 39–54.

Donoghue, S. (2000). Projective techniques in consumer research. *Journal of Family Ecology and Consumer Sciences, 28,* 47–53.

Falk, J. H., and Dierking, L. D. (2016). *The Museum Experience Revisited.* Taylor & Francis – Routledge: London.

Flint, D. J., Blocker, C. P., and Boutin, Jr., P. J. (2010). Customer value anticipation, customer satisfaction and loyalty: An empirical examination. *Industrial Marketing Management, 40,* 219–230.

Hanquinet, L. (2013). Visitors to modern and contemporary art museums: Towards a new sociology of cultural profiles. *The Sociological Review, 61*(4), 792–813.

Hooper-Greenhill, E. (1994). *Museums and Their Visitors.* Taylor & Francis – Routledge: London.

Holbrook, M. B., and Hirschman, E. C. (1982). The experiential aspects of consumption: Consumer fantasies, feelings, and fun. *Journal of Consumer Research, 9*(2), 132–140.

Holbrook, M. B., and Morris, B. (1999). *Consumer Value: A Framework for Analysis and Research.* Psychology Press: Hove, East Sussex.

Kotler, N. (2008). *Museum Marketing & Strategy: Designing Missions, Building Audiences, Generating Revenue & Resources.* Jossey-Bass: Hoboken, NJ.

Modesto, T., Ikeda, A., and Campomar, M. (2006). Laddering in the practice of marketing research: Barriers and solutions. *Qualitative Market Research: An International Journal, 9*(3), 297–306.

Morsch, C., and Holland, A. (2013). *Time for Cultural Mediation.* Accessed on July 29, 2022, Available at: https://prohelvetia.ch/app/uploads/2017/09/tfcm_0_complete_publication.pdf.

Reussner, M. (2003). Strategic management for visitor-oriented museums. *The International Journal of Cultural Policy, 9*(1), 95–108.

Ryan, A., Fenton, M., and Sangiorgi, D. (2010). A night at the theatre: Moving arts marketing from the office to the kitchen and beyond. In F. Kerrigan (Ed.), *Marketing the Arts: A Fresh Approach* (pp. 214–230). Taylor & Francis – Routledge: London.

Silverman, L. (1995). Visitors meaning making in museums for a new age. *Curator, 8*(3), 161–169.

Sheng, C., and Chen, M. (2011). A study of experience expectations of museum visitors. *Tourism Management, 33*(1), 53–60.

Styvén, M. E. (2010). The need to touch: Exploring the link between music involvement and tangibility preference. *Journal of Business Research, 63*(9/10), 1088–1094.

Tasci, A. (2016). A critical review of consumer value and its complex relationships in the consumer-based brand equity network. *Journal of Destination Marketing & Management, 5*(3), 171–191.

Taheri, B. (2011). *Unpacking Visitor Engagement: Examining Drivers of Engagement in Museums.* (Document n.T12995). [Doctoral dissertation, University of Strathclyde, Glasgow]. Accessed on July 29, 2022. Available at: https://stax.strath.ac.uk/concern/theses/zk51vg80x.

Varnum, E., and Grossmann, I. (2017). Cultural change: The how and the why. *Perspectives on Psychological Science, 12*(5), 1–17.

Weil, S. (1997). The museum and the public. *Museum Management and Curatorship, 16*(3), 257–271.

6 Museum Cultural Mediation as Transformative Museum Experience

Valeria Guerrisi

6.1 The Potential of Museum Cultural Mediation in the Post-Covid Era

If Marshal McLuhan (2017) had included the museum in his famous essay about media, he would probably have defined it as an extension of society. For this reason, the role and the notion of the museum itself are constantly evolving.

Is no news that the Covid-19 pandemic has been described as an epochal turning point in human history by the whole scientific community, who agrees that it will have long-term effects on twenty-first-century global society. Museums paid one of the highest prices since safety measures for the reduction of contagion have been inducing a striking impact on the public's relationship with cultural institutions, especially those whose consumption implies people's gathering (NEMO 2021; AAM 2022).

However, the pandemic has transformed almost every aspect of the work of museums and their professionals, forcing a massive – mostly digital – *call to action* which raised questions about the maturity and sustainability of these newly approached practices in the future (ICOM 2021).

Museums that survived, and even have benefited from this, are those characterized by a *transformative* approach long before this "great flood" arrived.

"Transformative museums" are those that ceaselessly question knowledge, information, and research by using all kinds of theoretical, practical, technological, and social approaches and evolve in terms of exhibition and education approaches, in terms of epistemological understandings, and terms of new practices and methods of communication (Nielsen 2014). The concept of "Transformative Museum" was used for the first time in 2012 as a conference title, held

DOI: 10.4324/9781003352754-6

by the Danish Research Centre on Education and Advanced Media Materials-DREAM. In those years, the postmodernist approach was leaving room for an even more flexible and participatory way of intending audience engagement. "Transformation" turned out to be a permanent condition of the society itself rather than something that cyclically happens, as Zygmunt Bauman's (2000) "Liquid Society" theorizes.

On the way to a *new normal* (Cowan et al. 2022), the pandemic taught museums to become more people-centric (Gallagher Nalls 2022) and more focused on a local dimension (ICOM 2021), either in a digital or analogical way. It is interesting how, in August 2022, ICOM updated the previous definition of Museum, dated 2007,[1] formalizing the cultural changes that probably were just boosted by the pandemic.

Concerning the previous version, greater attention is now paid to two aspects:

- The audience and its inclusion: "A museum is [...] Open to the public, accessible and inclusive, museums foster diversity and sustainability" (ICOM 2022).
- The social role of museums in shaping and be shaped by the community: "A museum is a not-for-profit, permanent institution in the service of society [...]. They operate and communicate ethically, professionally and with the participation of communities [...]" (ICOM 2022).

The – still very little – literature regarding the future of museums in the post-covid era agrees that the push to maintain and amplify remote relationships with the public with digital technologies will grant the very existence of museums and allow them to continue playing their social role (Lerario 2021). Nevertheless, in-person visits are still necessary for harbouring a sense of community and belonging (Gallagher Nalls 2022).

Museum cultural mediation is a service that can be functional in achieving ICOM's both goals. This emerging professional figure has increasingly proved its relevance in building audience engagement by bridging communication gaps and reducing the *distance* between visitors and the museum (Bulatova et al. 2020). Moreover, mediated tours allow visitors to feel an active part of the process, not only increasing their involvement but also their sense of responsibility in being part of a community. This kind of approach can be framed in the so-called "transformative education", whose implications will be further explored in the next chapter.

6.2 Museum Cultural Mediation as Transformative Educations

The process of transformative learning is based on the *Transformative theory* which was originally developed by Jack Mezirow in 1981. The theoretical premise is that adults have a coherent frame of reference that set automatically how they move from one specific activity (mental or behavioural) to another. This frame encompasses cognitive, conative, and emotional components and is composed of two dimensions: habits of mind and a point of view (Mezirow 1997). Transformative learning is the process of effecting change in consolidated a frame of reference. It is about the expansion of mindset and encouraging a reconsideration of one's worldview. As a side-effect, this approach to education may foster societal change by supporting critical thought (Bull 2020).

Transformative educators do not necessarily teach content that is remarkably different from more traditional educators. However, they are guided by different purposes and use different communication strategies when interacting with the learner (Dirks 1998).

This diversity in purpose is what marks the difference between a traditional tour guide and a museum cultural mediator.

M. Carolyn Clark (1993) affirms that different "strands" within the research and theory on transformative learning can be defined. John M. Dirkx (1998) identifies four main strands that correspond to as many important scholars in this field: as Paulo Freire, Larry Daloz, Robert Boyd, and Jack Mezirow.

These are namely:

• Transformation as Consciousness-raising
• Transformation as Development
• Transformation as Individuation
• Transformation as Critical Reflection

Transformation as Consciousness-raising. According to Freire (1970), transformative learning is consciousness-raising: he refers to it as "conscientization". Learning helps people develop a deeper understanding of how social structures shape and influence the way they think about themselves and the world.

They are "conscientious" about the way the world has shaped their frames of reference, and that they have the power to change those frames of reference by constructing their meaning of the world.

Transformation as Development. According to Daloz (1986), what motivates people to participate in learning experiences is the need to find and construct meaning within their lives. This ability is related to the developmental movement of our lives. The movement into new phases requires the learner to construct new meaning structures that help them perceive and make sense of their changing world. Transformative Learning for Daloz is more oriented to personal change than to social change. It deals more with the psychosocial and developmental context in which much of adult learning seems to take place (Dirkx, 1998).

Transformation as Individuation. Boyd (1991) works from the perspective of depth psychology, particularly the work of Carl Jung believed. According to him the emotional component, rather than the rational component of the transformational experience, is the major catalyst for change. Then, he believed the desired outcome of transformation is not autonomy, but a greater interdependent and compassionate relationship with other people (Dirkx 1998).

Boyd is more concerned with the expressive or emotional-spiritual dimensions of learning, and with integrating these dimensions holistically and consciously within our daily experience of life. He maintains that adult learners do this by making the unconscious conscious. This process is possible by using symbols images and metaphors which manage to elicit the most unconscious frames and establish an intrapersonal dialogue with them. In this regard, art can be particularly effective.

Transformation as Critical Reflection. Mezirow (Mezirow 2009; Henderson 2012; Taylor and Cranton, 2012) observes that we tend to have an urgent need to understand and order the meaning of our experience. The justification of what we know depends on the context in which our knowledge is embedded. By integrating the new meaning with what we know, we want to avoid the threat of chaos. Learning is understood as the process of using a prior interpretation to construe a new or revised interpretation of the meaning of one's experience as a guide to future action (Kitchener 1983 in Taylor and Cranton 2012). During the process of transformative learning, we modify our taken-for-granted frames of reference to make them more inclusive, discriminating, open, and emotionally capable of change and reflection.

If applied to the museum educational service, each of these strands can be useful in building a proper audience engagement strategy by leveraging the overall visitors' aims and values.

An engaged audience is a driver of a museum's success. Achieving this goal is only possible by profoundly knowing the targets, understanding their attitudes towards the institution, and taking advantage of the museum-owned touchpoints.

6.3 Fulfilling the Potential of Museum Cultural Mediation

A successful transformative customer journey is only possible through permanent attention to building a fulfilling relationship between an institution and its audience.

At this stage, it is important to understand which managerial actions should be implemented to fulfil the potential of museum cultural mediation.

Aspects to be defined are as follows:

1 Audience segmentation

When approaching a transformative learning experience, different audiences are moved by different purposes. Some want to be surprised and challenge their points of view, some want to get to know themselves, some other need to find their existential meaning, and others want control over reality. Audience segmentation is a fundamental first step to properly leveraging visitors' benefits and values.

Possible survey techniques will not be explored here but referring to the four-visitor profile presented in Chapter 4 is advised. Each profile shall be offered a unique experience: reinterpreted according to Product Life Cycle Theory (Levitt 1965), this customization strengthens audience loyalty and keeps engagement alive. During this initial analysis phase, great attention shall be paid to enlisting as many target visitors as possible by sponsoring the initiative on every channel relevant to the audience: this will also implicitly raise awareness of the mediation service.

2 An appropriate audience development strategy

Museums offer an existing global infrastructure, and their privileged position facilitates collective action by building networks, raising public awareness, and supporting knowledge creation and sharing for the long term (ICOM 2018).

When creating an audience development strategy, the museum needs to define first which role it wants to play as an institution, possibly maintaining a clear position on the socially relevant issue they wish to address.

Since a museum itself is a *medium,* and so are all its educational services, two key elements shall be clarified in advance: *what* it wants to communicate and to *whom.*

The four visitor profiles defined in the current research are strategic to customizing the right communication approach by associating each one with the mediator that best stimulates their interests and needs.

The communication strategy, including the communication style used by cultural mediators, must be consistent with the mission and the prevailing purpose of the museum among the four mentioned by ICOM's definition (namely *education, enjoyment, reflection, and knowledge sharing*). Certainly, a mediation visit can be geared towards several purposes all at once (e.g., to educate and entertain), or a museum may occasionally decide to adjust the tone depending on specific events or community. The most important aspect, however, is that every choice is made as a result of a clear *audience development strategy.*

An effective communication strategy is essential in creating the first touchpoint with the visitor, especially if the perceived distance (both cognitive and emotional) is the very barrier between the audience and the institution. This involves every aspect, from the curatorial project to labels, and even more so the mediators themselves. In particular, the *degree of participation* is an influential factor in the success of a museum's educational activities precisely because of the enhanced openness of the relationship. From a less to a more interactive visit, mediation can propose:

- A **receptive** approach: it is more like a *guided tour* and can be supported by other means of communication, such as brochures, leaflets, and catalogues.
- An **interactive** approach: the stimuli offered by the audience are central here. The mediator can engage the audience by *asking questions*, both relating to the content and personal feelings and emotions. The purpose of this is to familiarize the visitor with the topic and to allow a greater degree of personalization in understanding the information provided. Digital interaction can be integrated into this type of visit.
- A **participatory** approach: includes the possibility for visitors themselves *to produce* material, objects, and documents related to their experience. This is particularly useful for special categories, such as children or people with disabilities because they can learn by expressing themselves in a very personal way.

The interactive and participatory approaches are those that help the audience become aware and critical of their own and others' assumptions. As affirmed by the transformative education theory, using imagination helps with lateral thinking and the redefinition of certainties.

3 A proper organization and management of the educational service staff

Being a Transformative Museum requires a holistic approach that imbues the organization, the staff, and every output with a message coherent to the assumption by which the institution guide and support the single person and the community (McWhinney and Markos 2003). Cultural mediation programs and mediators are no exception.

This task is entrusted to the Head of Mediation and Educational Services who oversees all the programmes, actions, studies, and research projects that connect the works hosted within the museum to current and potential audiences (ICOM; ICTOP 2008). That means that he/she is the key individual that coordinates and implements every direct or indirect aspect concerning audience engagement by:

- Participating, under the responsibility of the Director, in the definition of policies for the public and defining actions about set target audiences.
- Cooperating with the Scientific Director of the museum in the related actions, planning, and introduction of material in support of exhibitions.
- Training mediators and guides and contributing also to the training of receptionists and custodians.
- Participating in the implementation of exhibitions.
- Implementing evaluation tools for programmes and educational actions.

A key aspect that needs to be addressed from the start is the organizational chart of the educational service staff. The Head of the service should establish how many and what kind of mediators are necessary by choosing among the four profiles mentioned in Chapter 2 (between Guide Mediator, Educator Mediator, Designer Mediator, and Manager Mediator).

Each profile has specific features that can be used in a different part of the process, from the management to the implementation of the exhibition, until – obviously – the visit itself. If the museum can benefit from an articulated managerial structure, it should involve different professional figures. In some successful cases, a partnership between institutions has led to shared management of the mediation service, thus optimizing human and economic resources and, at the same time, enriching the experience of the mediators themselves.

Tailoring the open positions to the institution's specific needs and goals is crucial. Although it may appear obvious, this research uncovered a lack of awareness around this figure and revealed that most calls for applications are very vague.

Every call for applications should be specific and differ from the others in terms of:

- Education
- Expertise
- Fieldwork
- Additional soft skills
- Communication skills (it is important to hire people that can speak more than one language)
- Activities and objectives, specifying the activities to be performed and whether the role is remunerated or not

According to these aspects, it is possible to summarize three different types of advertisements for selection:

- **Call for Guide Mediator**: requires a basic education with predominantly theoretical skills. It is not necessary to have prior fieldwork, so this profile is suitable for recruits.
- **Call for Educator Mediator/Designer Mediator:** requires transversal skills. Based on benchmarking among educational institutions, this profile requires a high-level academic background.
- **Call for Manager Mediator:** requires predominantly managerial skills. This profile, which calls for economic and legal knowledge, will be recruited among master's graduates at the university.

Different working agreements can be established, including volunteer work, internships, and grants. In any case, continuous collaboration with at least some key operators (e.g. with the mediator-manager) is recommended to build a solid organization conducive to continual development.

Should this possibility arise, a steady partnership between museums and educational institutions can bring mutual advantages. For instance, they can work together in organizing proper preparatory training with a view to internships.

Furthermore, the quality of the mediation service depends on well-structured internal knowledge sharing. The National Gallery of Modern and Contemporary Art of Rome has proved to be a "leading case" in this field. This museum, which can count on more than fifteen cultural mediators available in shifts at various times, organized an internal hierarchy between the Senior (with at least one year of experience at the institution) and Junior (newly hired). Junior mediators benefit from dedicated internal training courses (directed by the manager and other mediators) and early on are joined on visits by veterans. Moreover, the Head of Mediation and Educational Services supervises field operators' activities and knows each one in-depth. The relationship between the audience and the mediator during the visit is fundamental and it would be wise not to consider the operatives interchangeable (for example, some might be more inclined to conduct visits with children, others with adults). For this reason, the assignment of every single tour is customized accordingly to their respective features and talents.

4. Customized visit duration and tour itinerary

Depending on the level of knowledge and interest, the mediator may propose itineraries aimed at exploring specific topics or may propose an in-depth focus on artists or artistic movements.

In this regard, it is possible to match the four strands with a specific profile of the visitor, to structure a pleasant, customized experience.

- **Transformation as Consciousness-raising for the curious visitor**

  Consciousness-raising is level 0 of transformative learning. This visitor experience museum cultural mediation for the first time and cannot count on a solid knowledge of the subject matter. Seeking entertainment, his goal is to have a pleasant and stimulating experience.

  The mediator can foster critical consciousness among the visitors by making them develop the ability to analyse contexts that influence and shape the content of the exhibition also implicitly leveraging a comparison whit their own lives. Visitors must be encouraged to pose questions and be active co-creator of the tour. This may raise their awareness about being active participants also in the social, political, cultural, economic, contexts and many others.

- **Transformation as Development for the passionate visitor**

  The passionate visitor is driven by a curiosity about the subject and its innovativeness. He possesses sufficient knowledge of the topic and returns to the same museum several times to deepen their knowledge. They are attracted by hedonism and the enrichment of their cultural background. Approaching the same topic from a different point of view "can serve to disrupt old patterns of meaning and encourage the construction and formation of new ways of seeing the self and the world"

(Dirkx, 1998). For the Passionate visitor, it is useful to structure shorter and well-suited tours, preferably thematic and emotional, with more opportunities to discuss and enjoy the exhibition.

- **Transformation as Individuation for the involved visitor**
  In search of hedonism, involved visitors wish to have extremely moving experiences, to learn what kinds of feelings and emotions the arts arouse in them. For this purpose, the mediator's role is essential: especially through art, images, symbols, and metaphors that may be used to elicit deep-seated issues and concerns, at an unconscious level. Through these processes, learners gain insight into those aspects of themselves that remain hidden from conscious awareness yet serve to influence and shape their sense of self, and their interpretations of their external world (Khabanyane et al. 2014).

- **Transformation as Critical Reflection for the expert visitor**
  The expert visitor includes a very deep and broad cultural background. Moreover. They are constantly in search of new knowledge and want to discover different opinions and divergent perspectives on works of art. The main goal of expert visitors is to open their minds, and this is why they are interested in museum cultural mediation. In this regard, they desire to integrate previous knowledge with new meaning to revise or have a new interpretation of an already known topic. For the Expert visitor, who has already visited the museum several times and would not return except for a special event, periodic or occasional visits should be set up. Directly involving experts would mean a more focused tour, carried out in shorter time frames (required by this kind of visitor), and centred on a specific topic (Figure 6.1).

The importance of *a feedback touch-point system* is also stressed. A continuous flow of information from the audience allows the Head of Mediation to obtain all the elements necessary to make the service increasingly tailored. This feedback shall come from the visitors both in an informal way (asking questions during and after the tour) and in a structured way (through surveys, questionnaires, etc.). Lastly, feedback can also come from the mediators themselves.

Another aspect that should not be underestimated is the need to boost the mediation service. With it being a growing professional figure, most people do not even know about its existence. A dual approach is recommended; the first one is to act locally, advertising the service

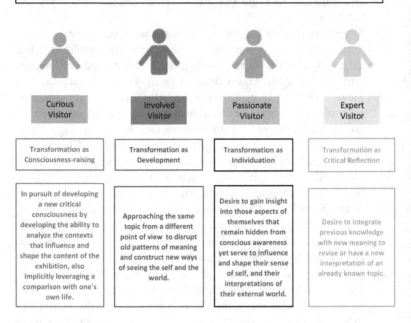

Figure 6.1 Visitors' strands of transformative museum cultural mediation experience.

Source: Our elaboration.

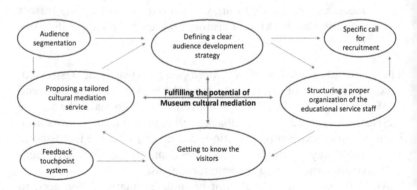

Figure 6.2 Managerial indications flowchart.

Source: Our elaboration.

within the museum itself by displaying posters, distributing brochures about mediation, and using a specific uniform to induce curiosity in the visitor. A wider audience could then be reached through social media and websites. This task should be coordinated with all the professional figures involved in communication (such as the social media manager, the press officer, etc.) (Figure 6.2).

6.4 Future Perspectives: Potential for Museum Cultural Mediation in the Post-Covid Era

The conceptualization of the Transformational Museum is not new (Nielsen 2014) but at the dawn of the so-called Post-covid Era appears newly relevant.

In a few years, the way people think about the role and responsibility of museums in bringing social change has evolved. Although the idea remains controversial, museums are increasingly seen as a key intellectual and civic resource to address future global challenges (Janes and Sandell 2019). The pandemic had the effect of boosting and consolidating this idea and ICOM's new definition of museums is evidence of this.

Transformative education services may help achieve this goal, but it will only be successful if museums can unite to acknowledge their role as agents of positive change (Bull 2020).

In support of the delivery of these transformational experiences, Bull (2020) suggests a three-step process that here will be adapted to museum cultural mediation:

1. Ensure that the organization and the educational programs maintain a clear position on the socially relevant issues they wish to address. To bring real impact the organization shall embed these values through its mission and vision (ICOM 2018). The more the focus is clear, the more institutions will be able to embrace the new requirements of our ever-changing society and act quickly. This topic may occasionally be addressed when specific mediated tours and events occur.
2. Conceptualize learning experiences that help visitors become aware and critical of their own and others' assumptions. Not only do objects, digital and live programming, artworks, and immersive experiences all can unlock new perspectives (Hooper-Greenhill 2013), but also museum cultural mediation has great potential in opening a discussion for transformation.

According to a constructivist approach (Hein 1995), transformative museum cultural mediation experiences shall:
- Know the starting mindset and previous experience of the visitor.
- Address a deep or diverse understanding of the topic. This will naturally lead to the rising of new ideas and maybe hint at new possibilities.
- Challenge previous mindsets and paradigms by leveraging these new possibilities.
- Support the internalization of these new perspectives so they can be converted into new habits and organization of the idea.
3. Challenge long-term success by sharing results, refining the offer, and repeating. Institutions adopting museum cultural mediation would benefit from collaborating in sharing best practices and in the development of an evaluative framework that adopts external accreditation systems, as suggested by the American Alliance of Museums in the report *Museums, Environmental Sustainability, and Our Future.*

The strength of governance and the skills of the museum professionals are the key elements that can steer the sector into a brand new phase, outward-focused and socially active (Janes and Sandell 2019). This attitude will pose significant challenges for the future as museums have the potential to understand complex issues in advance and convey thoughtful, creative, and transformative experiences. In short, they can make a difference.

Note

1 ICOM definition of Museum, 2007: Museum is a non-profit, permanent institution in the service of society and its development, open to the public, which acquires, conserves, researches, communicates, and exhibits the tangible and intangible heritage of humanity and its environment for education, study, and enjoyment.

Reference list

American Alliance of Museums – AAM. (2013). "Museums, Environmental Sustainability and Our Future". Accessed on September 24, 2022. Available at: http://ww2.aam-us.org/docs/default-source/professional-networks/picgreenwhitepaperfinal.pdf
American Alliance of Museums – AAM. "National Snapshot of COVID-19 Impact on United States Museums. January 2022. Accessed on September 24, 2022. Available at: https://www.aam-us.org/2022/02/08/national-snapshot-

of-covid-19-impact-on-united-states-museums-fielded-december-2021-january-2022/

Bauman, Z. (2000). *Liquid Modernity*. Polity Press: Cambridge.

Bull, J. D. (2020). '...Threat and Opportunity to Be Found in the Disintegrating World.' (O'Hara 2003, 71) – The potential for transformative museum experiences in the post-covid era. *Journal of Conservation and Museum Studies*, *18*(1), 3.

Boyd, R. (1991). *Personal Transformation in Small Groups: A Jungian Perspective*. Taylor & Francis – Routledge: London.

Bulatova, A., Melnikova, S., and Zhuravleva, N. (2019). *The Significance of Art Mediation in Bridging the Communication Gaps*. KnE publishing: Dubai. Accessed on June 20, 2022. Available at: https://knepublishing.com/index.php/KnE-Social/article/view/6355/11743.

Clark, M. C. (1993). Transformational learning. In S. B. Merriam (Ed.), *An Update on Adult Learning Theory* (pp. 47–56). Jossey-Bass: San Francisco, CA. (New Directions for Adult and Continuing Education, 57).

Cowan, E., et al. (2022) A new normal: Assessment outcomes and recommendations for virtual versus in-person curricula in post-COVID-19 times. *Medical Science Educator* 32(2), 379–387.

Daloz, L. (1986). *Effective Teaching and Mentoring: Realizing the Transformational Power of Adult Learning Experiences*. Jossey-Bass: San Francisco, CA.

Danish Research Centre on Education and Advanced Media Materials – DREAM. (2013). "The Transformative Museum Conference". Accessed on September 23, 2022. Available at: http://www.dreamconference.dk/

Dirkx, J. M. (1998). Transformative learning theory in the practice of adult education: An overview. *PAACE Journal of Lifelong Learning, 7*, 1–14.

Freire, P. (1970). *Pedagogy of the Oppressed*. Seabury Press: New York.

Gallagher Nalls, A. (2022). Crafting a post-disaster experience: How visitor experience staff have adapted to the pandemic. American Alliance of Museums – AAM. Accessed on September 24, 2022. Available at: https://www.aam-us.org/2022/02/18/crafting-a-post-disaster-experience-how-visitor-experience-staff-have-adapted-to-the-pandemic/

Henderson, J. (2012). Transformative learning: Four activities that set the stage. Fostering a climate conducive to transformative learning. *Faculty Focus, 17*, 1–5.

Hein, G. (1995). The constructivist museum. *Journal for Education in Museums, 16*, 21–23.

Hooper-Greenhill, E. (2013). *Museums and Their Visitors*. Routledge: Oxford.

ICOM International Committee for the Training of Personnel (ICTOP). Ruge, A. (dir.). (2008). Museum professions – a European frame of reference. ICOM International Committee for the Training of Personnel: Berlin.

ICOM. (2018). ICOM establishes a new working group on sustainability. Accessed on September 24, 2022. Available at: https://icom.museum/en/news/icom-establishes-new-working-group-on-sustainability/

ICOM. (2021). Museums, museum professionals, and Covid-19. Third survey. Accessed on September 24, 2022. Available at: https://icom.museum/wp-content/uploads/2021/07/Museums-and-Covid-19_third-ICOM-report.pdf

Janes, R., and Sandell, R. (eds.) (2019). *Museum Activism*. Routledge: London.

Khabanyane, K. E., Maimane, J. R., and Ramabenyane, M. J. (2014). A critical reflection on transformative learning as experienced by student-teachers during school-based learning. *Mediterranean Journal of Social Sciences, 5*(27), 452–459. MCSER Publishing: Rome.

Kotler, et al. (2008). *Museum Marketing and Strategy: Designing Missions, Building Audiences, Generating Revenue and Resources*. John Wiley & Sons: Hoboken, NJ.

Levitt, T. (1965). Exploit the product life cycle. *Harvard Business Review, 43*(6), 62–70.

Lerario, A. (2021). Languages and context issues of ICTs for a new role of museums in the COVID-19 Era. *Heritage, 4*(3065–3080), 1–16.

Lyotard, J.F. (1984). *The Postmodern Condition. A Report on Knowledge*. Manchester University Press: Manchester.

McWhinney, W., and Markos, L. (2003). Transformative education: Across the threshold. *Journal of Transformative Education, 1*(1), 16–37.

McLuhan, M. (2017). *Understanding Media. The Extension of Man*. Ginko Press: Berkeley, CA.

Mezirow, J. (1997). *Transformative Learning: Theory to Practice. New Directions for Adult and Continuing Education, 74*. Jossey-Bass Publishers: Hoboken, NJ.

Network of European Museum Organization – NEMO. (2021). "Follow-up survey on the impact of Covid-19 on museum in Europe. Final Report". Accessed on September 14, 2022. Available at: https://www.nemo.org/fileadmin/Dateien/public/NEMO_documents/NEMO_COVID19_FollowUpReport_11.1.2021.pdf

Nielsen, J. (2014). Transformations in the postmodern museum. *Museological Review, 18*, 22–29.

Silberman, N. A. (2021). Good-bye to all that: COVID-19 and the transformations of cultural heritage. *International Journal of Cultural Property*. Cambridge University Press. Accessed on September 24, 2022. Available at: https://www-cambridge-org.biblio-proxy.uniroma3.it/core/journals/international-journal-of-cultural-property/article/goodbye-to-all-that-covid19-and-the-transformations-of-cultural-heritage/58D28A8996B73CA5301D1EBE8CAA2285

Taylor, E. W., and Cranton, P. a. A. (2012). *The Handbook of Transformative Learning. Theory, Research, and Practice*. Jossey-Bass: San Francisco, CA.

Wimmer, C. (2010). Exchange die Kunst, Musik zu vermitteln: Qualitäten in der Musikvermittlung und Konzertpädagogik. Accessed on September 14, 2022. Available at: http://www.miz.org/downloads/dokumente/569/2010_Studie-Die_Kunst-Musik-zu-vermitteln_Stiftung-Mozarteum-Salzburg.pdf

Index

Note: **Bold** page numbers refer to tables; *italic* page numbers refer to figures and page numbers followed by "n" denote endnotes.

Printed in the United States
by Baker & Taylor Publisher Services